Paleo: 30 Day Paleo Challenge:

Unlock The Secret To Health And Dramatic Weight Loss With The Paleo Diet 30 Day Challenge

Complete 30 Day Paleo Cookbook

By Luca Fontaine

30 DAY PALEO CHALLENGE

Legal notice

Table of Contents

INTRODUCTION...10
Day 1...13
BREAKFAST: Paleo Warm Turkey Fritters...............................13
LUNCH: Nutritious Mixed Salads...16
DINNER: Spiced Beef Stew with Carrots and Blueberries.........19
Day 2...22
BREAKFAST: Tasty Pork Meatballs in Tomato Sauce...............22
LUNCH: Red and Green Paleo Salads.......................................25
DINNER: Traditional Indian Curry...28
Day 3...31
BREAKFAST: Paleo Crunchy Cereal...31
LUNCH: Delicious Paleo Chicken With Sweet Potato Chips.....34
DINNER: Grilled Chicken Spicy...38
Day 4...41
BREAKFAST: Smooth Coconut Carrot Pudding.......................41
LUNCH: Original Steamed Broccoli...44
DINNER: Spicy Beef and Butternut Squash Stew.....................47
Day 5...50
BREAKFAST: The Nutritious Spinach Omelet..........................50
LUNCH: Energetic Veggie Tuna Salads....................................53
DINNER: Delicious Simple Baked Salmon...............................56
Day 6...59
BREAKFAST: Delicious Coconut Pancake with Strawberry
Sauce...59
LUNCH: Simple Tomato Red Soup..62
DINNER: Spicy Chicken Kebab...65
Day 7...68
BREAKFAST: Scrumptious Macadamia Paleo Waffles.............68
LUNCH: Nutritious Mixed Salads...71
DINNER: Delicious Pork in Blanket...74

Day 8...77
BREAKFAST: Delectable Ginger Banana Paleo Bars...............77
LUNCH: Jalapeno Chicken in Lettuce Tacos............................80
DINNER: Tasteful Savory Shrimp Stew....................................83
Day 9...86
BREAKFAST: Spicy Vegetable Casserole.................................86
LUNCH: Paleo Salads in Jar...89
DINNER: Scrumptious Spicy Paleo Pork Ribs.........................92
Day 10...95
BREAKFAST: Paleo Simple Almond Muffin.............................95
LUNCH: Blue Banana Paleo Muffin..98
DINNER: Original Beef Patties with Scrumptious Sauce.........101
Day 11...105
BREAKFAST: Paleo Warm Turkey Fritters.............................105
LUNCH: Red and Green Paleo Salads....................................108
DINNER: Delicious Pork in Blanket.......................................111
Day 12...114
BREAKFAST: Tasty Pork Meatballs in Tomato Sauce............114
LUNCH: Energetic Veggie Tuna Salads..................................117
DINNER: Original Steamed Broccoli......................................120
Day 13...123
BREAKFAST: Paleo Crunchy Cereal.......................................123
LUNCH: Sweet Cashew Paleo Brownie...................................126
DINNER: Tasteful Savory Shrimp Stew..................................129
Day 14...132
BREAKFAST: Smooth Coconut Carrot Pudding.....................132
LUNCH: Delicious Paleo Chicken With Sweet Potato Chips...135
DINNER: Scrumptious Spicy Paleo Pork Ribs.......................139
Day 15...142
BREAKFAST: The Nutritious Spinach Omelet.........................142
LUNCH: Simple Tomato Red Soup...145
DINNER: Original Beef Patties with Scrumptious Sauce.........148
Day 16...152
BREAKFAST: Delicious Coconut Pancake with Strawberry

Sauce..152
LUNCH: Nutritious Mixed Salads.................................155
DINNER: Spiced Beef Stew with Carrots and Blueberries.......158
Day 17...161
BREAKFAST: Scrumptious Macadamia Paleo Waffles............161
LUNCH: Jalapeno Chicken in Lettuce Tacos...........................164
DINNER: Grilled Chicken Spicy...167
Day 18...170
BREAKFAST: Delectable Ginger Banana Paleo Bars..............170
LUNCH: Paleo Salads in Jar...173
DINNER: Spicy Beef and Butternut Squash Stew..................177
Day 19...180
BREAKFAST: Spicy Vegetable Casserole.............................180
LUNCH: Red and Green Paleo Salads....................................183
DINNER: Delicious Simple Baked Salmon............................186
Day 20...189
BREAKFAST: Paleo Simple Almond Muffin.........................189
LUNCH: Energetic Veggie Tuna Salads.................................192
DINNER: Delicious Pork in Blanket.......................................195
Day 21...198
BREAKFAST: Paleo Warm Turkey Fritters...........................198
LUNCH: Original Steamed Broccoli.......................................201
DINNER: Spicy Chicken Kebab..204
Day 22...207
BREAKFAST: Tasty Pork Meatballs in Tomato Sauce............207
LUNCH: Delicious Paleo Chicken With Sweet Potato Chips...210
DINNER: Tasteful Savory Shrimp Stew.................................214
Day 23...217
BREAKFAST: Paleo Crunchy Cereal.....................................217
LUNCH: Simple Tomato Red Soup..220
DINNER: Delicious Pork in Blanket.......................................223
Day 24...226
BREAKFAST: Smooth Coconut Carrot Pudding....................226
LUNCH: Jalapeno Chicken in Lettuce Tacos..........................229

DINNER: Scrumptious Spicy Paleo Pork Ribs..........................232
Day 25...235
BREAKFAST: The Nutritious Spinach Omelet.......................235
LUNCH: Red and Green Paleo Salads....................................238
DINNER: Original Beef Patties with Scrumptious Sauce.........241
Day 26...245
BREAKFAST: Delicious Coconut Pancake with Strawberry
Sauce..245
LUNCH: Energetic Veggie Tuna Salads.................................248
DINNER: Traditional Indian Curry.......................................251
Day 27...254
BREAKFAST: Scrumptious Macadamia Paleo Waffles...........254
LUNCH: Delicious Paleo Chicken With Sweet Potato Chips...257
DINNER: Spiced Beef Stew with Carrots and Blueberries.......261
Day 28...264
BREAKFAST: Delectable Ginger Banana Paleo Bars.............264
LUNCH: Paleo Salads in Jar..267
DINNER: Grilled Chicken Spicy..271
Day 29...274
BREAKFAST: Spicy Vegetable Casserole.............................274
LUNCH: Original Steamed Broccoli.....................................277
DINNER: Delicious Simple Baked Salmon............................280
Day 30...283
BREAKFAST: Paleo Simple Almond Muffin.........................283
LUNCH: Nutritious Mixed Salads..286
DINNER: Spicy Chicken Kebab...289

INTRODUCTION

For the last several years, few diets have grown with the speed that the Paleo diet has. In a short period of time Paleo has become a mainstream and popular diet for people from all walks of life. One of the reasons for its popularity is that Paleo is not just a great weight loss diet. Paleo is so much more. Paleo is a lifestyle that promotes maximum health, energy, and longevity. It is the healthiest and most natural way for us to eat. This is because the Paleo diet is simply based on the natural way of eating that sustained humanity for generations.

You may wonder how people in the paleolithic era managed their health and physical fitness without the presence of modern doctors, nutritionists, and the various technological innovations in health and nutrition science. Healthiness standards were not so well developed and they completely relied on what was presented to them by nature. Simply put, the foods that they ate (and perhaps more importantly the foods that they *didn't* eat) is the secret to the superior health of paleolithic man.

Fortunately, we can learn from the success of our ancestors and enjoy the same healthy diet they did. This is the purpose of the Paleo diet. The Paleo diet is based on eating healthy, unprocessed food that is found in nature. Fresh produce, simple cooking techniques, and good honest food is what Paleo is all about.

Beyond the health and weight loss benefits of Paleo, one of the diet's greatest features is the wide range of delicious food that is Paleo compliant. You can be fully Paleo while still eating plenty of meat, fruits, vegetables, seafood, nuts, seeds, and healthy fats.

This diversity of food enables people to eat deliciously, fulfill their appetites, and *still* lose impressive amounts of weight at the same time. Furthermore, the various Paleo food options ensure that you can easily get the complete nutrition you need for healthy living. Many other dieting methods prohibit you from eating meat, suggest avoiding all fats, or write off entire macronutrient categories. The Paleo diet on the other hand permits you to enjoy all kinds of food which makes it an easy diet to stick to for life. No one likes force-feeding themselves bland and tasteless food and the Paleo diet ensures you don't have to suffer to get the health and weight loss results you want.

Losing weight using the Paleo diet means that you will be consuming plenty of lean protein such as chicken and seafood. Besides that, it is also recommended that you enjoy lots of multicolor vegetables that are eaten raw, steamed or otherwise cooked in a simple way. Some healthy fats like avocado and olive oil are also an important part of the Paleo diet, as are unsalted nuts such as macadamia, walnuts, almond, and pecans. Though fruits can be tasty and healthy, some fruits have a high sugar content. If weight loss is your goal, you will want to limit your fruit intake and focus mostly on vegetables. Feel free to consume fruits once or twice a day as a snack or dessert however.

While you are on a Paleo diet you can expect to consume fruits, vegetables, lean meat, nuts, and eggs. Almost all meat is Paleo. For example poultry, steak, and pork are Paleo. The exception however is that you will want to avoid any kinds of processed meat like hot dogs, spam, and other low-quality meat that paleolithic man did not have access to. Fish are absolutely an essential part of the Paleo diet as they contain important vitamins, minerals, and nutrients, such as omega-3. Pretty much anything you can pull out of the sea is Paleo. If it swims and has fins, it is

Paleo. Crab, shrimp, clams, lobster, scallop, and oyster are also fully Paleo compliant foods. Vegetables are of course an important part of Paleo as well. Other kinds of food that are allowed in Paleo are healthy fat, nuts, and fruits.

Though Paleo diet permits you to consume a diverse menu of food options, there are some kinds of food that you will have to say goodbye to. The Paleo diet prohibits the consumption of dairy, soft drinks, grains, and legumes. Commercially produced "fruit juice" is also forbidden as it contains high sugar and little to no actual fruit. Any artificial sweetener or preservative is prohibited as well. This may be a big change for some, but the mouth-watering recipes in this book should provide a relatively easy transition.

Simply start at day 1 of the meal plan and follow it through to day 30. You'll enjoy a full month of amazing Paleo recipes your whole family will love. Paleo is a diet that can change your life. Every single recipe in this book has been tried and tested in my own kitchen and served to audiences around the world. From the award-winning Paleo Warm Turkey Fritter, to the mega-popular Tasty Pork Meatballs in Tomato Sauce, to the simple Paleo Crunchy Cereal, and the amazing Smooth Coconut Carrot Pudding, each and every Paleo recipe in this book is designed to delight the taste buds while promoting maximum health, longevity, energy, and weight loss. You will not feel like you are on a diet this month. Instead, you will feel fitter, healthier, and happier – I guarantee it!

Day 1

BREAKFAST: Paleo Warm Turkey Fritters

30 DAY PALEO CHALLENGE

Serving: 6

Nutrition Facts
Serving Size 3 g

Amount Per Serving
Calories 22
Calories from Fat 21
% Daily Value*
Total Fat 2.4g
4%
Cholesterol 0mg
0%
Sodium 0mg
0%
Potassium 8mg
0%
Total Carbohydrates 0.5g
0%
Protein 0.1g

| Vitamin A 0% | • | Vitamin C 0% |
| Calcium 0% | • | Iron 1% |

Nutrition Grade C-
* Based on a 2000 calorie diet

14

Ingredients:
- 2 cups chopped roasted turkey
- 1 teaspoon minced garlic
- 1 teaspoon ginger powder
- 1 teaspoon minced rosemary
- ½ teaspoon black pepper powder
- 3 teaspoons olive oil

Instructions:
- Place chopped roasted turkey, minced garlic, ginger powder, minced rosemary, and black pepper powder in a food processor.
- Process until well combined then form the mixture into small patty shape—about 10 patties.
- Preheat a saucepan and pour olive oil into the saucepan.
- Once it is hot, arrange the patties on the saucepan and cook for a few minutes.
- Flip the patties and make sure the both sides are lightly brown.
- Transfer the cooked patties on a serving dish and enjoy warm.

LUNCH: Nutritious Mixed Salads

Serving: 3

Nutrition Facts

Serving Size 66 g

Amount Per Serving

Calories 31

Calories from Fat 2

% Daily Value*

Total Fat 0.2g

0%

Trans Fat 0.0g

Cholesterol 0mg

0%

Sodium 165mg

7%

Potassium 122mg

3%

Total Carbohydrates 7.7g

3%

Dietary Fiber 1.0g

4%

Sugars 5.5g

Protein 0.6g

Vitamin A 19%	•	Vitamin C 49%
Calcium 2%	•	Iron 4%

Nutrition Grade A

* Based on a 2000 calorie diet

Ingredients:
- 1 cup chopped spinach
- 1 cup shredded sea bass
- 1 cup chopped pineapple
- ½ cup chopped half ripe papaya
- ½ teaspoon cumin
- ¼ teaspoon black pepper powder

Instructions:
- Steam the bass until cooked then set aside.
- Layer spinach, pineapple, papaya, and steamed sea bass in a salad bowl.
- Season with cumin and pepper then serve right away.

DINNER: Spiced Beef Stew with Carrots and Blueberries

Serving: 3

Nutrition Facts

Serving Size 96 g

Amount Per Serving

Calories 152

Calories from Fat 112

% Daily Value*

Total Fat 12.4g

19%

Saturated Fat 1.6g

8%

Trans Fat 0.0g

Cholesterol 0mg

0%

Sodium 182mg

8%

Potassium 209mg

6%

Total Carbohydrates 10.1g

3%

Dietary Fiber 2.2g

9%

Sugars 5.1g

Protein 1.9g

Vitamin A 123%	•	Vitamin C 12%
Calcium 3%	•	Iron 4%

Nutrition Grade B+

* Based on a 2000 calorie diet

Ingredients:
- 2 cups chopped beef
- ½ cup fresh blueberries
- 1 cup chopped carrots
- 1 tablespoon almond butter
- 2 tablespoons olive oil
- ¼ teaspoon sea salt
- ¼ teaspoon black pepper
- ¼ teaspoon garlic powder
- ½ cup sliced onion

Instructions:
1. Preheat a skillet then pour olive oil into the skillet.
2. Once it is hot, stir in chopped beef and onion then sauté until the onion is aromatic and the beef is wilted.
3. Season the beef with sea salt, black pepper powder, and garlic powder.
4. Add the chopped carrots and cook stir until cooked.
5. Last, add in the blueberries and butter then stir until the butter melts.
6. Transfer the cooked beef to a serving dish and serve warm.

Day 2

BREAKFAST: Tasty Pork Meatballs in Tomato Sauce

30 DAY PALEO CHALLENGE

Serving: 6

Nutrition Facts
Serving Size 28 g

Amount Per Serving
Calories 15
Calories from Fat 7
% Daily Value*
Total Fat 0.8g
1%
Trans Fat 0.0g
Cholesterol 0mg
0%
Sodium 6mg
0%
Potassium 29mg
1%
Total Carbohydrates 1.2g
0%
Sugars 0.5g
Protein 0.8g

Vitamin A 0%   •   Vitamin C 1%
Calcium 0%   •   Iron 0%
Nutrition Grade B+
* Based on a 2000 calorie diet

Ingredients:

- 1 ½ cups chopped pork
- 1 organic egg white
- ½ cup chopped onion
- 3 teaspoons coconut flour
- 1 teaspoon olive oil
- ¾ teaspoon ginger powder
- 1 cup mashed tomato
- 4 tablespoons water
- 2 teaspoons apple cider vinegar
- ¼ teaspoon garlic powder

Instructions:

1. First, make the sauce by combining mashed tomato, water, apple cider vinegar, garlic powder, and ¼ teaspoon ginger powder in a pot then bring to a simmer. Set aside.
2. Next, preheat an oven to 350 °F and line a baking pan with parchment paper. Set aside.
3. Meanwhile, place the chopped pork, egg white, onion, coconut flour, olive oil, and ginger powder together with ginger powder in a food processor.
4. Process until well combined and shape into small meatballs.
5. Arrange the meatballs on the prepared baking pan and bake for approximately 12 minutes.
6. Transfer the baked meatballs to a serving dish then pour sauce over the meatballs.
7. Serve and enjoy immediately.

LUNCH: Red and Green Paleo Salads

30 DAY PALEO CHALLENGE

Serving: 3

Nutrition Facts
Serving Size 124 g

Amount Per Serving
Calories 103
Calories from Fat 86
% Daily Value*
Total Fat 9.6g
15%
Saturated Fat 1.4g
7%
Trans Fat 0.0g
Cholesterol 0mg
0%
Sodium 3mg
0%
Potassium 186mg
5%
Total Carbohydrates 5.0g
2%
Dietary Fiber 1.2g
5%
Sugars 1.8g
Protein 0.9g

Vitamin A 5%	•	Vitamin C 7%
Calcium 4%	•	Iron 6%

Nutrition Grade C+

Ingredients:
- 1 teaspoon minced garlic
- 3 teaspoons sliced basil
- 3 teaspoons chopped oregano
- 1 medium cucumber
- 2 tablespoons chopped red tomato
- 2 tablespoons balsamic vinegar
- 2 tablespoons olive oil
- 1 teaspoon black pepper powder

Instructions:
1. Cut the cucumber into cubes and discard the seeds. Set aside.
2. Toss the cubed cucumber, tomato, minced garlic, sliced basil, and chopped oregano in a salad bowl.
3. Drizzle balsamic vinegar and olive oil over the vegetable mixture then sprinkle black pepper powder on top.
4. Serve and enjoy.

DINNER: Traditional Indian Curry

30 DAY PALEO CHALLENGE

Serving: 3

Nutrition Facts
Serving Size 154 g

Amount Per Serving
Calories 159
Calories from Fat 70
% Daily Value*
Total Fat 7.8g
12%
Saturated Fat 2.6g
13%
Trans Fat 0.0g
Cholesterol 43mg
14%
Sodium 317mg
13%
Potassium 303mg
9%
Total Carbohydrates 3.7g
1%
Dietary Fiber 0.9g
4%
Sugars 1.4g
Protein 19.0g

| Vitamin A 2% | • | Vitamin C 3% |
| Calcium 3% | • | Iron 8% |

Nutrition Grade B
* Based on a 2000 calorie diet

Ingredients:
- 1 teaspoon olive oil
- 1 tablespoon chopped onion
- ¼ teaspoon pepper powder
- ½ cup cubed sweet potatoes
- 1 teaspoon curry powder
- 1 teaspoon tomato paste
- ½ teaspoon ginger powder
- 1 ½ teaspoons garlic powder
- 1 cup chicken broth
- ½ tablespoon tomato
- 2 tablespoons coconut milk
- 1 cup chopped chicken breast
- 1 ½ teaspoons almond butter
- 2 tablespoons cilantro

Instructions:
1. Preheat olive oil in a skillet then stir in chopped onion. Sauté until wilted and aromatic then add the cubed sweet potatoes into the skillet.
2. Stir until the sweet potatoes soften and season with pepper powder.
3. Add curry powder, tomato paste, ginger powder, and garlic powder into the skillet then pour chicken broth over the seasoned sweet potatoes.
4. Put chopped chicken breast into the skillet together with the almond butter and cilantro.
5. Bring to boil and stir until the chicken is completely cooked.
6. Transfer the curry to a serving bowl and serve warm.

Day 3

BREAKFAST: Paleo Crunchy Cereal

30 DAY PALEO CHALLENGE

Serving: 5

Nutrition Facts
Serving Size 3 g

Amount Per Serving
Calories 10
Calories from Fat 9
% Daily Value*
Total Fat 1.0g
1%
Saturated Fat 0.6g
3%
Cholesterol 0mg
0%
Sodium 0mg
0%
Potassium 11mg
0%
Total Carbohydrates 0.4g
0%
Protein 0.2g

Vitamin A 0%	Vitamin C 0%
Calcium 0%	Iron 2%
Nutrition Grade B+	

* Based on a 2000 calorie diet
Nutrition Facts

Ingredients:
- 2 tablespoons shredded coconut
- 1 tablespoon sunflower seeds
- 1 ½ teaspoons chia seeds
- 1 teaspoon cinnamon powder
- 1 small egg white

Instructions:
1. Preheat an oven to 325 °F and line a baking pan with parchment paper.
2. Combine all ingredients in a food processor then process until well combined and become dough.
3. Place the dough on a flat surface then roll until you have a rectangle with 1/4 –inch thick.
4. Cut the dough into 1/2 –inch x 1/2 –inch squares then arranges them on the prepared baking pan.
5. Bake for approximately 25 minutes until the squares are lightly brown.
6. Transfer to a serving bowl and enjoy.

LUNCH: Delicious Paleo Chicken With Sweet Potato Chips

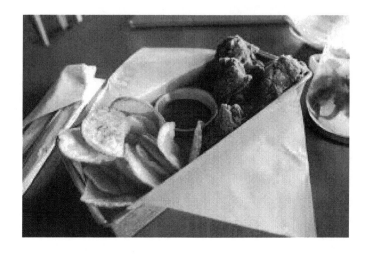

Serving: 2

Nutrition Facts
Serving Size 210 g

Amount Per Serving
Calories 720
Calories from Fat 536
% Daily Value*
Total Fat 59.5g
92%
Saturated Fat 13.7g
69%
Cholesterol 54mg
18%
Sodium 1001mg
42%
Potassium 419mg
12%
Total Carbohydrates 29.4g
10%
Dietary Fiber 2.5g
10%
Sugars 4.5g
Protein 21.6g

| Vitamin A 8% | • | Vitamin C 32% |
| Calcium 2% | • | Iron 18% |

Nutrition Grade C
* Based on a 2000 calorie diet

Ingredients:
POTATO CHIPS
- 1 medium sweet potato
- 3 teaspoons olive oil
- 1 teaspoon chopped rosemary
- ½ teaspoon sea salt

CRISPY CHICKEN
- 1 cup chopped chicken
- 4 tablespoons tapioca starch
- ½ teaspoon sea salt
- ¼ teaspoon black pepper powder
- ¼ teaspoon paprika
- ¼ teaspoon garlic powder
- ½ cup olive oil

Instructions:
1. Preheat an oven to 375 °F. Prepare a baking pan then line with parchment paper. Set aside.
2. Peel the sweet potato and slice thinly using a very sharp knife.
3. Season the sliced sweet potato with olive oil, chopped rosemary, and sea salt.
4. Arrange the sweet potato on the prepared baking pan then bake for about 10 minutes.
5. Flip each sliced potato and return to the oven for another 10 minutes. The sweet potato chips will look golden brown.
6. Transfer the sweet potato chips to a bowl then set aside.
7. Reduce the oven to 350 °F. Prepare another baking pan and line with parchment paper. Set aside.
8. Combine tapioca starch, sea salt, black pepper powder, paprika, and garlic powder in bowl. Stir well.
9. Coat the chicken with the mixture then refrigerate for

approximately 15 minutes.
10. Preheat a skillet then pour olive oil into the skillet.
11. Once it is hot, fry the coated chicken for about 3 minutes.
12. Flip the chicken and fry for another 3 minutes until both sides of the chicken are golden brown.
13. Transfer the fried chicken on the prepared baking pan and bake for about 20 minutes.
14. Arrange the baked chicken and potato chips in a lunch box and enjoy at lunch.

DINNER: Grilled Chicken Spicy

Servings: 2

Nutrition Facts

Serving Size 350 g

Amount Per Serving

Calories 1,286

Calories from Fat 1018

% Daily Value*

Total Fat 113.1g

174%

Saturated Fat 15.0g

75%

Trans Fat 0.0g

Cholesterol 194mg

65%

Sodium 981mg

41%

Potassium 719mg

21%

Total Carbohydrates 4.0g

1%

Dietary Fiber 2.0g

8%

Sugars 0.8g

Protein 73.8g

Vitamin A 45%	•	Vitamin C 8%
Calcium 5%	•	Iron 23%

Nutrition Grade C+

* Based on a 2000 calorie diet

Ingredients:
- 1 lb. chicken breast
- 1 cup olive oil, to fry
- 1 tablespoon sweet paprika
- 1 teaspoon chili powder
- ¾ teaspoon sea salt
- ½ teaspoon allspice
- 1 teaspoon black pepper powder
- 1 ½ teaspoon olive oil
- 1 teaspoon minced garlic
- 1 teaspoon tomato paste
- 1 tablespoon lime juice
- Lemon slices, for garnish

Instructions:
1. Cut the chicken breast into slices. Set aside.
2. Place sweet paprika, chili powder, sea salt, allspice, black pepper powder, olive oil, minced garlic, tomato paste, and lime juice in a bowl. Stir well.
3. Add the chicken into the mixture and marinate for at least 30 minutes.
4. Preheat a grill over medium heat. Once it is hot, cook the chicken for approximately 4 minutes then flips it. Make sure that both sides of the chicken are golden brown.
5. Remove the chicken from the grill and transfer to a serving dish.
6. Garnish with lemon slices and enjoy.

Day 4

BREAKFAST: Smooth Coconut Carrot Pudding

Serving: 3

Nutrition Facts
Serving Size 200 g

Amount Per Serving
Calories 49
Calories from Fat 27
% Daily Value*
Total Fat 3.0g
5%
Trans Fat 0.0g
Cholesterol 0mg
0%
Sodium 30mg
1%
Potassium 159mg
5%
Total Carbohydrates 4.5g
2%
Dietary Fiber 1.1g
4%
Sugars 1.8g
Protein 1.4g

Vitamin A 123%	•	Vitamin C 4%
Calcium 3%	•	Iron 2%

Nutrition Grade A
* Based on a 2000 calorie diet

Ingredients:
- 1 cup chopped carrots
- 2 cups water
- 3 teaspoons coconut butter
- 3 teaspoons almond butter
- ¼ teaspoon cinnamon powder
- ¼ teaspoon nutmeg powder

Instructions:
1. Pour water in a pan and bring to boil.
2. Once it is boiled, add in the chopped carrots then cook for approximately 15 minutes until tender.
3. Drain the cooked carrots and place into a food processor.
4. Add the remaining ingredients into the food processor then puree until smooth and creamy.
5. Transfer the mixture to a serving bowl and enjoy right away.

LUNCH: Original Steamed Broccoli

Serving: 1

Nutrition Facts
Serving Size 142 g

Amount Per Serving
Calories 325
Calories from Fat 232
% Daily Value*
Total Fat 25.7g
40%
Saturated Fat 2.2g
11%
Trans Fat 0.0g
Cholesterol 0mg
0%
Sodium 31mg
1%
Potassium 655mg
19%
Total Carbohydrates 16.3g
5%
Dietary Fiber 6.3g
25%
Sugars 2.6g
Protein 12.8g

Vitamin A 11%   •   Vitamin C 137%
Calcium 18%   •   Iron 14%
Nutrition Grade A-
* Based on a 2000 calorie diet

Ingredients:
- 1 cup broccoli florets
- 1 teaspoon minced garlic
- 4 tablespoons chopped almonds
- 1 ½ tablespoons almond butter

Instructions:
1. Pour water in a small saucepan and bring to boil.
2. Once it is boiled, toss in the broccoli and cook for a few seconds. Drain and place in a bowl.
3. Preheat the saucepan over medium heat then stir in almond butter, minced garlic, and chopped almonds.
4. Sauté them well until the almond butter melts and the garlic is lightly golden brown.
5. Drizzle almond butter on the top of the broccoli and serve right away.

DINNER: Spicy Beef and Butternut Squash Stew

Serving: 1

Nutrition Facts
Serving Size 606 g

Amount Per Serving
Calories 182
Calories from Fat 129
% Daily Value*
Total Fat 14.4g
22%
Saturated Fat 2.1g
11%
Trans Fat 0.0g
Cholesterol 0mg
0%
Sodium 93mg
4%
Potassium 437mg
12%
Total Carbohydrates 14.5g
5%
Dietary Fiber 4.2g
17%
Sugars 6.5g
Protein 1.5g

Vitamin A 387%	•	Vitamin C 15%
Calcium 8%	•	Iron 6%

Nutrition Grade B+
* Based on a 2000 calorie diet

Ingredients:
- 1 tablespoon olive oil
- 2 cups cubed beef
- 1 teaspoon minced garlic
- 2 teaspoons minced sage
- ¼ teaspoon smoked paprika
- 1 tablespoon chopped red chilies
- 2 cups cubed butternut squash
- 1 cup chopped carrots
- 2 cups water
- ¼ teaspoon pepper powder

Instructions:
1. Preheat olive oil in a Dutch oven over medium heat. Once it is hot, brown the cubed beef until half cooked and wilted. Set aside.
2. Toss the minced garlic, sage, chopped red chilies and smoked paprika in the skillet then season with pepper powder.
3. Return the cooked beef into the skillet together with cubed butternut squash and carrots then pour water over the beef.
4. Bring to boil then reduce the heat and cook for an hour or more until the beef is tender.
5. Transfer the stew to a serving bowl then enjoy hot.

Day 5

BREAKFAST: The Nutritious Spinach Omelet

30 DAY PALEO CHALLENGE

Serving: 4

Nutrition Facts
Serving Size 43 g

Amount Per Serving
Calories 47
Calories from Fat 32
% Daily Value*
Total Fat 3.6g
5%
Saturated Fat 0.5g
3%
Trans Fat 0.0g
Cholesterol 0mg
0%
Sodium 23mg
1%
Potassium 93mg
3%
Total Carbohydrates 2.0g
1%
Sugars 0.8g
Protein 2.2g

Vitamin A 14%	•	Vitamin C 6%
Calcium 1%	•	Iron 1%

Nutrition Grade B
* Based on a 2000 calorie diet

Ingredients:
- 1 tablespoon olive oil
- ½ cup chopped onion
- 1 teaspoon minced garlic
- 1 cup chopped spinach
- 2 organic egg whites
- ¼ teaspoon black pepper powder

Instructions:
1. Preheat a skillet over medium heat then pour olive oil into the skillet.
2. Once it is hot, stir in chopped onion and dice garlic into the skillet then sauté until wilted and lightly golden brown. Set aside.
3. Place the egg whites and beat them in a medium bowl. After that, put the sautéed onion and garlic then add the remaining ingredients into the beaten eggs.
4. Preheat an oven to 350 °°F and line a baking pan with parchment paper.
5. Pour the egg mixture into the prepared baking pan and bake for approximately 15 minutes until lightly brown.
6. Transfer the baked omelet to a serving dish then serve immediately.
7. Best to be enjoyed with tomato sauce.

LUNCH: Energetic Veggie Tuna Salads

30 DAY PALEO CHALLENGE

Servings: 4

Nutrition Facts
Serving Size 11 g

Amount Per Serving

Calories 3

Calories from Fat 0

% Daily Value*

Total Fat 0.0g

0%

Trans Fat 0.0g

Cholesterol 0mg

0%

Sodium 7mg

0%

Potassium 40mg

1%

Total Carbohydrates 0.7g

0%

Protein 0.2g

| Vitamin A 7% | • | Vitamin C 9% |
| Calcium 1% | • | Iron 1% |

Nutrition Grade A

* Based on a 2000 calorie diet

Ingredients:
- ¼ cup cooked tuna chunks
- ¼ cup chopped celery
- ¼ cup chopped parsley
- 1 teaspoon minced garlic
- ½ teaspoon black pepper powder

Instructions:
1. Place all ingredients in a salad bowl.
2. Using a fork mix all ingredients until combined.
3. Cover the salad bowl with a lid then chill in the refrigerator for at least an hour or more.
4. Enjoy cold.

DINNER: Delicious Simple Baked Salmon

Serving: 2

Nutrition Facts
Serving Size 244 g

Amount Per Serving

Calories 365

Calories from Fat 190

% Daily Value*

Total Fat 21.1g

33%

Saturated Fat 3.1g

15%

Trans Fat 0.0g

Cholesterol 100mg

33%

Sodium 336mg

14%

Potassium 889mg

25%

Total Carbohydrates 0.8g

0%

Protein 44.2g

Vitamin A 5%	•	Vitamin C 7%
Calcium 10%	•	Iron 15%

Nutrition Grade C+

* Based on a 2000 calorie diet

Ingredients:
- 1 lb. salmon fillet
- 1 tablespoon lemon juice
- ¼ teaspoon sea salt
- ¼ teaspoon black pepper powder
- 2 teaspoons chopped thyme
- 1 tablespoon olive oil

Instructions:
1. Preheat an oven to 400 °F then lines a baking pan with parchment paper.
2. Place salmon on the prepared baking pan then season with salt and black pepper.
3. Next, splash lemon juice over the salmon and sprinkle thyme on top.
4. After that, drizzle with olive oil and bake for approximately 25 minutes.
5. Once it is done, remove the cooked salmon from the oven then transfer to a serving dish.
6. Serve immediately.

Day 6

BREAKFAST: Delicious Coconut Pancake with Strawberry Sauce

30 DAY PALEO CHALLENGE

Serving: 6

Nutrition Facts
Serving Size 21 g

Amount Per Serving
Calories 24
Calories from Fat 21
% Daily Value*
Total Fat 2.4g
4%
Trans Fat 0.0g
Cholesterol 0mg
0%
Sodium 1mg
0%
Potassium 61mg
2%
Total Carbohydrates 1.1g
0%
Sugars 0.6g
Protein 0.1g

| Vitamin A 0% | • | Vitamin C 12% |
| Calcium 2% | • | Iron 0% |

Nutrition Grade C+
* Based on a 2000 calorie diet

Ingredients:
- ¼ cup coconut flour
- 4 fresh organic eggs white
- 2 ½ tablespoons water
- 3 teaspoons olive oil
- ½ teaspoon baking powder
- ¼ teaspoon apple cider vinegar
- ½ cup fresh strawberries
- Fresh strawberries, for garnish

Instructions:
1. Combine coconut flour and eggs whites in a bowl.
2. Using a hand mixer beat them until smooth and creamy then adds water and olive oil into the mixture.
3. Meanwhile, preheat a saucepan over low heat.
4. Stir in baking powder and apple cider vinegar a few seconds before pouring the mixture into the hot saucepan.
5. Take about ¼ cup of the mixture and pour into the hot saucepan. Cook for approximately 30 seconds then flip the pancake.
6. Make sure that both sides of the pancake are lightly golden brown.
7. Repeat to the remaining mixture and set aside.
8. After that, place fresh strawberries in a blender then blend on high speed until creamy and incorporated.
9. Put a pancake on a serving dish and coat with strawberry sauce.
10. Cover with another pancake and repeat with the remaining pancakes and strawberry sauce.
11. Garnish with fresh strawberries and serve immediately.

LUNCH: Simple Tomato Red Soup

30 DAY PALEO CHALLENGE

Serving: 3

Nutrition Facts

Serving Size 14 g

Amount Per Serving

Calories 20

Calories from Fat 14

% Daily Value*

Total Fat 1.6g

2%

Cholesterol 0mg

0%

Sodium 3mg

0%

Potassium 38mg

1%

Total Carbohydrates 1.6g

1%

Sugars 0.6g

Protein 0.3g

| Vitamin A 1% | • | Vitamin C 3% |
| Calcium 1% | • | Iron 1% |

Nutrition Grade B

* Based on a 2000 calorie diet

Ingredients:
- 2 medium red tomatoes
- ¼ cup chopped onion
- 1 teaspoon minced garlic
- 1 teaspoon olive oil
- 1 teaspoon chopped parsley
- ¾ cup vegetable stock
- 1 teaspoon tomato paste
- ¼ teaspoon pepper powder

Instructions:
1. Preheat an oven to 350 °F. Prepare a baking pan and line with parchment paper. Set aside.
2. Cut the red tomatoes into wedges then arrange on the prepared baking pan.
3. Place onion and minced garlic among the tomatoes then splash olive oil over the tomatoes and onion.
4. Sprinkle pepper and chopped parsley on the top then bake for approximately 40 minutes. The tomatoes will reduce for approximately half their size.
5. Remove the baked ingredients from the oven and set aside.
6. Combine vegetable stock with tomato paste in a pan then bring to boil.
7. Add the baked ingredients into the vegetable stock and bring to a simmer for approximately 10 minutes.
8. Let it stand for a few minutes and when it is warm, transfer the mixture to a blender.
9. Blend until smooth and incorporated and pour into a serving bowl.
10. Garnish with fresh parsley on top then serve warm.

DINNER: Spicy Chicken Kebab

30 DAY PALEO CHALLENGE

Serving: 2

Nutrition Facts
Serving Size 40 g

Amount Per Serving
Calories 237
Calories from Fat 230
% Daily Value*
Total Fat 25.5g
39%
Saturated Fat 3.6g
18%
Trans Fat 0.0g
Cholesterol 0mg
0%
Sodium 85mg
4%
Potassium 14mg
0%
Total Carbohydrates 4.8g
2%
Sugars 4.4g
Protein 0.4g

Vitamin A 0%	•	Vitamin C 0%
Calcium 0%	•	Iron 1%

Nutrition Grade D
* Based on a 2000 calorie diet

Ingredients:
- 1 lb. boneless chicken breast without fat
- ¼ cup olive oil
- 3 teaspoons yellow mustard
- ½ tablespoon raw honey
- Lemon slices, for garnish
- Lettuce, for garnish

Instructions:
1. Combine olive oil, yellow mustard, and raw honey in a bowl.
2. Cut the boneless chicken into cubes.
3. Skewer the cubed chicken with wooden skewers then grease with the sauce.
4. Preheat a grill pan and once it is hot, grill the chicken over medium heat until completely cooked.
5. Repeat to grease the chicken with sauce during the grilling process.
6. Arrange the grilled chicken on a serving dish and garnish with fresh lettuce and sliced lemon.
7. Serve and enjoy warm.

Day 7

BREAKFAST: Scrumptious Macadamia Paleo Waffles

30 DAY PALEO CHALLENGE

Serving: 5

Nutrition Facts
Serving Size 23 g

Amount Per Serving

Calories 56
Calories from Fat 52

% Daily Value*

Total Fat 5.8g
9%
Saturated Fat 0.9g
4%
Cholesterol 0mg
0%
Sodium 58mg
2%
Potassium 30mg
1%
Total Carbohydrates 0.8g
0%
Protein 1.0g

Vitamin A 0%	•	Vitamin C 0%
Calcium 1%	•	Iron 1%

Nutrition Grade C+

* Based on a 2000 calorie diet

Nutrition Facts

Serving Size 23 g

69

Ingredients:
- 1 organic egg white
- 4 tablespoons chopped macadamia nuts
- 2 teaspoons olive oil
- 3 teaspoons coconut flour
- ¼ teaspoon baking soda
- ¼ cup water

Instructions:

1. Place all of the ingredients in a bowl. Using a hand mixer beat until smooth and incorporated.
2. Preheat a waffle iron over low heat then pour the mixture into the hot waffle iron.
3. Cook for approximately 45 minutes then transfer the waffles to a serving dish..
4. Best to be served with unsweetened fruit juice as healthy breakfast.

LUNCH: Nutritious Mixed Salads

Serving: 3

Nutrition Facts
Serving Size 66 g

Amount Per Serving
Calories 31
Calories from Fat 2
% Daily Value*
Total Fat 0.2g
0%
Trans Fat 0.0g
Cholesterol 0mg
0%
Sodium 165mg
7%
Potassium 122mg
3%
Total Carbohydrates 7.7g
3%
Dietary Fiber 1.0g
4%
Sugars 5.5g
Protein 0.6g

Vitamin A 19%	•	Vitamin C 49%
Calcium 2%	•	Iron 4%

Nutrition Grade A
* Based on a 2000 calorie diet

Ingredients:
- 1 cup chopped spinach
- 1 cup shredded sea bass
- 1 cup chopped pineapple
- ½ cup chopped half ripe papaya
- ½ teaspoon cumin
- ¼ teaspoon black pepper powder

Instructions:
1. Steam the bass until cooked then set aside.
2. Layer spinach, pineapple, papaya, and steamed sea bass in a salad bowl.
3. Season with cumin and pepper then serve right away.

DINNER: Delicious Pork in Blanket

30 DAY PALEO CHALLENGE

Serving: 1

Nutrition Facts
Serving Size 0 g

Amount Per Serving
Calories 0
Calories from Fat 0
% Daily Value*
Total Fat 0.0g
0%
Cholesterol 0mg
0%
Sodium 0mg
0%
Potassium 0mg
0%
Total Carbohydrates 0.0g
0%
Protein 0.0g

Vitamin A 0%   •
Calcium 0%   •
Nutrition Grade C+
* Based on a 2000 calorie diet

Vitamin C 0%
Iron 0%

Ingredients:
- 1 lb. pork meat without fat
- 2 cups homemade barbecue sauce
- 12 slices bacon
- Fresh chopped lettuce, chopped cabbage, and lemon slices for garnish

Instructions:
1. Cut the pork into 6 medium cubes then place in a bowl with a lid.
2. Pour barbecue sauce over the cubed pork and marinate for at least 8 hours or overnight.
3. Place two slices of bacon on a flat surface then put a cube of pork on the top of the bacon.
4. Carefully wrap the pork with bacon then secure with a toothpicks.
5. Repeat with the remaining ingredients.
6. Preheat a grill over medium heat.
7. Once it is hot, grill the wrapped pork then flips until the pork is no longer pink and completely cooked.
8. Arrange the grilled pork on a serving dish and serve with fresh cabbage, lettuce, and lemon slice.
9. Enjoy right away.

Day 8

BREAKFAST: Delectable Ginger Banana Paleo Bars

Serving: 8

Nutrition Facts
Serving Size 20 g

Amount Per Serving
Calories 52
Calories from Fat 39
% Daily Value*
Total Fat 4.3g
7%
Cholesterol 0mg
0%
Sodium 80mg
3%
Potassium 57mg
2%
Total Carbohydrates 3.6g
1%
Sugars 1.8g
Protein 0.2g

Vitamin A 0%	•	Vitamin C 2%
Calcium 0%	•	Iron 0%

Nutrition Grade C+
* Based on a 2000 calorie diet

Nutrition Facts
Serving Size 20 g

Ingredients:
- 1 medium ripe banana
- ½ cup almond flour
- 2 ½ tablespoons almond oil
- 3 organic eggs whites
- ¾ teaspoon ginger powder
- 1 teaspoon cinnamon powder
- ½ teaspoon cardamom
- ½ teaspoon baking soda

Instructions:
1. Preheat an oven to 350 °F and line a small baking pan with parchment paper.
2. Peel the banana and cut into slices.
3. Place the sliced banana in a food processor together with almond oil, eggs whites, ginger powder, cinnamon powder, and cardamom. Process until smooth and incorporated.
4. Add in the baking soda then quickly stir until well combined.
5. Pour the mixture into the prepared baking pan and bake for approximately 30 minutes.
6. Once it is done, remove from the oven and let it cool for about 30 minutes.
7. Cut into bars and arrange on a serving dish.
8. Serve and enjoy.

LUNCH: Jalapeno Chicken in Lettuce Tacos

Serving: 4

Nutrition Facts
Serving Size 104 g

Amount Per Serving
Calories 109
Calories from Fat 71
% Daily Value*
Total Fat 7.9g
12%
Saturated Fat 1.0g
5%
Trans Fat 0.0g
Cholesterol 16mg
5%
Sodium 143mg
6%
Potassium 227mg
6%
Total Carbohydrates 3.9g
1%
Dietary Fiber 1.0g
4%
Sugars 2.3g
Protein 6.8g

| Vitamin A 12% | • | Vitamin C 17% |
| Calcium 1% | • | Iron 4% |

Nutrition Grade B+
* Based on a 2000 calorie diet

Ingredients:
- ½ cup chicken strips
- 2 tablespoons olive oil
- ¼ cup chopped onion
- 1 ½ cup chopped tomatoes
- 1 tablespoon jalapeno chili
- ½ teaspoon cumin
- ¼ teaspoon brown sugar
- ¼ teaspoon sea salt
- ¼ teaspoon pepper powder
- Fresh lettuce leaves, for the tacos
- 1 tablespoon chopped leek
- 1 tablespoon sliced jalapeno chilies

Instructions:
1. Preheat a skillet then pour olive oil into the skillet.
2. Once it is hot, stir in chicken strips and fry until golden brown. Set aside.
3. In the same skillet, sauté the chopped onion until wilted and aromatic then add chopped tomatoes, jalapeno chilies, cumin, brown sugar, sea salt, and pepper powder. Bring to a simmer for approximately 15 minutes until the mixture is thicken.
4. Return the chicken into the sauce and cook for another 5 minutes.
5. Prepare a fresh lettuce on a flat surface then put a scoop of cooked chicken and sauce on the lettuce.
6. Sprinkle chopped leek and sliced jalapeno chili then carefully wrap with the lettuce.
7. Repeat to the remaining lettuce and chicken and arrange on a serving dish.
8. Serve and enjoy.

DINNER: Tasteful Savory Shrimp Stew

Serving: 1

Nutrition Facts
Serving Size 384 g

Amount Per Serving
Calories 166
Calories from Fat 132
% Daily Value*
Total Fat 14.7g
23%
Saturated Fat 2.5g
13%
Cholesterol 0mg
0%
Sodium 24mg
1%
Potassium 212mg
6%
Total Carbohydrates 8.7g
3%
Dietary Fiber 2.1g
8%
Sugars 4.0g
Protein 1.5g

Vitamin A 9%	•	Vitamin C 66%
Calcium 4%	•	Iron 2%

Nutrition Grade C+
* Based on a 2000 calorie diet

Ingredients:
- ¾ cup fresh shrimps
- 1 teaspoon grated lime zest
- 1 teaspoon grated lemon zest
- 4 tablespoons lime juice
- 4 tablespoons lemon juice
- 4 tablespoons cilantro
- 3 teaspoons olive oil
- ½ cup chopped onion
- 1 teaspoon minced garlic
- 1 teaspoon red chili flakes
- ¼ teaspoon cayenne pepper

Instructions:
1. Place half of the lemon and lime zest in a bowl with a lid.
2. Add cilantro and stir until incorporated.
3. Put the shrimps into the mixture and marinate for approximately 30 minutes.
4. Place the olive oil in a soup pot over medium heat. Once it is hot, stir in chopped onion and minced garlic into the pot and sauté until wilted and aromatic.
5. Add in red chili flakes, water, and cayenne pepper into the pot then bring to a simmer.
6. After that, add the marinated shrimps into the pot and cook for approximately 6 minutes.
7. Transfer the shrimp stew to a serving bowl and garnish with sprigs of leaf.
8. Enjoy hot.

Day 9

BREAKFAST: Spicy Vegetable Casserole

30 DAY PALEO CHALLENGE

Serving: 6

Nutrition Facts
Serving Size 27 g

Amount Per Serving

Calories 16
Calories from Fat 7
% Daily Value*
Total Fat 0.8g
1%
Trans Fat 0.0g
Cholesterol 0mg
0%
Sodium 17mg
1%
Potassium 71mg
2%
Total Carbohydrates 1.9g
1%
Dietary Fiber 0.6g
2%
Sugars 0.6g
Protein 0.5g

Vitamin A 12% • Vitamin C 16%
Calcium 1% • Iron 2%
Nutrition Grade A

* Based on a 2000 calorie diet
Nutrition Facts

Ingredients:
- 1 cup chopped spinach
- ½ cup broccoli florets
- 1 teaspoon olive oil
- ½ cup chopped onion
- 1 tablespoon chopped green chili
- 1 teaspoon minced garlic
- 2 organic eggs whites, lightly beaten
- ¼ teaspoon black pepper powder
- 1 tablespoon chopped parsley, for garnish

Instructions:
1. Preheat an oven to 375 °F and grease a small casserole dish with cooking spray.
2. Preheat a skillet then pour olive oil into the skillet.
3. Once it is hot, stir in chopped onion, minced garlic and green chilies into the skillet and sauté until wilted and aromatic.
4. Transfer the sautéed onion mixture to the beaten eggs then season with black pepper powder.
5. Add the chopped spinach and broccoli florets into the egg mixture and stir well.
6. Pour the mixture into the prepared casserole dish then bake for approximately 45 minutes.
7. Once it is cooked, remove the casserole from the oven and let it cool for about five minutes.
8. Sprinkle chopped parsley on the top for garnish.
9. Serve and enjoy warm.

LUNCH: Paleo Salads in Jar

Serving: 2

Nutrition Facts
Serving Size 144 g

Amount Per Serving
Calories 100
Calories from Fat 45
% Daily Value*
Total Fat 5.0g
8%
Saturated Fat 0.9g
4%
Trans Fat 0.0g
Cholesterol 16mg
5%
Sodium 135mg
6%
Potassium 329mg
9%
Total Carbohydrates 8.2g
3%
Dietary Fiber 2.1g
9%
Sugars 4.0g
Protein 6.3g

Vitamin A 112%	•	Vitamin C 60%
Calcium 3%	•	Iron 7%

Nutrition Grade A
* Based on a 2000 calorie diet

Ingredients:
- 1 ½ teaspoons olive oil
- ¼ cup chopped chicken fillet
- ½ cup sliced carrots
- ½ cup sliced bell pepper
- ¼ cup chopped onion
- 1 teaspoon minced garlic
- ¼ cup mashed avocado
- 1 tablespoon lime juice
- 2 tablespoons salsa
- 2 tablespoons chopped tomato
- ½ cup cubed cucumber
- ¼ cup chopped cilantro
- 1 cup chopped fresh lettuce

Instructions
1. Preheat a skillet then pour half of the olive oil into the skillet.
2. Once it is hot, stir in chopped chicken fillet and cook until golden brown.
3. Set aside.
4. In the same skillet, pour the remaining olive oil then cooks the sliced carrot until tender.
5. Add the sliced bell pepper, onion, and garlic then sauté for a few minutes. Turn the stove off.
6. Combine mashed avocado and lime juice until incorporated then set aside.
7. Place salsa in the bottom of the jar and spread evenly.
8. Layer with avocado mixture, continued with cooked vegetables, then put chicken over the vegetables.
9. Add chopped tomato and cucumber then place cilantro and fresh lettuce on top.
10. Cover the jar with the lid then refrigerate until you want to

consume it.
11.　　Enjoy!

DINNER: Scrumptious Spicy Paleo Pork Ribs

Serving: 1

Nutrition Facts
Serving Size 148 g

Amount Per Serving

Calories 901

Calories from Fat 901

% Daily Value*

Total Fat 101.7g

156%

Saturated Fat 14.6g

73%

Cholesterol 0mg

0%

Sodium 29mg

1%

Potassium 185mg

5%

Total Carbohydrates 7.7g

3%

Dietary Fiber 3.1g

12%

Sugars 1.7g

Protein 1.4g

Vitamin A 40%   •

Calcium 5%   •

Vitamin C 13%

Iron 9%

Nutrition Grade D+

Ingredients:

- 2 lb. pork rib without fat
- ½ tablespoon minced garlic
- ¼ cup chopped onion
- 1 teaspoon paprika
- 1 teaspoon coriander
- 1 teaspoon oregano
- 1 teaspoon red chili powder
- ½ cup olive oil
- ½ teaspoon cinnamon powder
- Lemon slices, for garnish

Instructions:

1. Combine minced garlic, chopped onion, paprika, coriander, oregano, and red chili powder in a bowl. Stir until incorporated.
2. Rub the pork rib with the mixture and marinate for approximately 30 minutes.
3. Preheat an oven to 300 °F and prepare a baking pan.
4. Wrap the marinated pork rib with aluminum foil then place on the baking pan and bake for 60 minutes.
5. Meanwhile, combine the olive oil with cinnamon powder, set aside.
6. Remove the cooked pork rib from the oven and discard the aluminum foil.
7. Grease the cooked pork with applesauce mixture then return into the oven and bake for another 30 minutes.
8. Once it is done, remove from the oven then transfer to a serving dish.
9. Garnish with lemon slices then serve hot.

Day 10

BREAKFAST: Paleo Simple Almond Muffin

Serving: 4

Nutrition Facts
Serving Size 18 g

Amount Per Serving
Calories 65
Calories from Fat 61
% Daily Value*
Total Fat 6.8g
10%
Saturated Fat 0.6g
3%
Trans Fat 0.0g
Cholesterol 0mg
0%
Sodium 88mg
4%
Potassium 16mg
0%
Total Carbohydrates 0.3g
0%
Protein 0.9g

Vitamin A 0%   •   Vitamin C 0%
Calcium 0%   •   Iron 0%
Nutrition Grade D+
* Based on a 2000 calorie diet
Nutrition Facts

Ingredients:
- 2 tablespoons almond flour
- 2 tablespoons almond oil
- 1 organic egg white
- 1 ½ teaspoons unsweetened apple juice
- ¼ teaspoon baking soda
- ½ teaspoon apple cider vinegar
- Roasted sliced almonds, for garnish

Instructions:
1. Preheat an oven to 350 °F and prepare 3 muffin paper cups.
2. Place almond flour, almond oil, and egg whites in a bowl. Stir until smooth and incorporated.
3. Pour unsweetened apple juice into the mixture then baking soda, and apple cider vinegar into the mixture.
4. Stir until well combined then divide the mixture into 3 muffin paper cups.
5. Sprinkle sliced almond on the top then bake for approximately 20 minutes or until a toothpick comes out clean.
6. Remove the muffins from the oven and let them cool for about 30 minutes.
7. Serve and enjoy.

LUNCH: Blue Banana Paleo Muffin

30 DAY PALEO CHALLENGE

Serving: 6

Nutrition Facts
Serving Size 34 g

Amount Per Serving
Calories 75
Calories from Fat 49
% Daily Value*
Total Fat 5.4g
8%
Saturated Fat 0.6g
3%
Cholesterol 0mg
0%
Sodium 110mg
5%
Potassium 162mg
5%
Total Carbohydrates 5.7g
2%
Dietary Fiber 0.7g
3%
Sugars 2.5g
Protein 1.9g

Vitamin A 0%   •   Vitamin C 3%
Calcium 3%   •   Iron 2%
Nutrition Grade B+

* Based on a 2000 calorie diet

Ingredients:
- 1 ripe banana
- 1 organic egg white
- 2 tablespoons almond butter
- 3 teaspoons olive oil
- 2 tablespoons coconut flour
- ½ teaspoon cinnamon powder
- ½ teaspoon baking soda
- ½ teaspoon baking powder
- 2 tablespoons blueberries

Instructions:
1. Peel the banana then mash it until smooth.
2. Place the mashed banana in a bowl then combine with egg white, almond butter, and olive oil.
3. Stir in coconut flour, cinnamon powder, baking powder, and baking soda then mix well.
4. Add the blueberries and stir until just combined.
5. Preheat an oven to 350 F. Prepare 8 muffin paper cups
6. Pour the muffin batter into 8-muffin paper cups then bake for approximately 25 minutes.
7. Bake for approximately 15 minutes then remove the muffins from the oven.
8. Place the muffin in a serving dish and enjoy.

DINNER: Original Beef Patties with Scrumptious Sauce

30 DAY PALEO CHALLENGE

Serving: 1

Nutrition Facts
Serving Size 552 g

Amount Per Serving
Calories 1,905
Calories from Fat 1905
% Daily Value*
Total Fat 211.7g
326%
Saturated Fat 30.4g
152%
Trans Fat 0.0g
Cholesterol 0mg
0%
Sodium 71mg
3%
Potassium 594mg
17%
Total Carbohydrates 20.4g
7%
Dietary Fiber 5.2g
21%
Sugars 8.4g
Protein 4.5g

Vitamin A 7%	•	Vitamin C 24%
Calcium 19%	•	Iron 19%

Nutrition Grade D

Ingredients:
PATTIES
- ¼ cup chopped onion
- 1 teaspoon olive oil
- 1 cup minced beef
- ¼ cup grated beetroot
- 1 teaspoon diced garlic
- 1 tablespoon chopped rosemary
- 1 teaspoon black pepper powder
- 1 cup olive oil, for frying
- 1 cup sliced cucumber

CUCUMBER SALADS
- 1 cup sliced cucumber
- 1 teaspoon lemon zest
- 3 teaspoons sesame seeds
- 2 tablespoons apple cider vinegar
- ½ teaspoon Dijon mustard
- ¼ teaspoon black pepper powder

GARNISH
- Fresh lettuce
- Fresh parsley

Instructions:
1. Preheat a skillet then pour olive oil into the skillet.
2. Once it is hot, stir in onion and sauté until wilted and aromatic.
3. Place the sautéed onion together with the patties ingredients in a bowl and mix well.
4. Using your hands, mold the mixture into small patties.
5. Preheat a frying pan then pour a cup of olive oil into the pan.
6. Once it is hot, arrange the patties on the pan and cook for

approximately 6 minutes.

7. Carefully flip the patties and cook another side for 6 minutes as well—the beetroot can easily burn so avoid high heat in frying the patties.

8. Once the patties are cooked, remove from the pan and let them cool for a few minutes.

9. Meanwhile, combine the salad ingredients in a bowl and mix until incorporated.

10. Arrange fresh lettuce on a serving dish then put the patties on the lettuce.

11. Drizzle sauce over the patties and garnish with fresh parsley.

12. Serve and enjoy at dinner.

Day 11

BREAKFAST: Paleo Warm Turkey Fritters

30 DAY PALEO CHALLENGE

Serving: 6

Nutrition Facts
Serving Size 3 g

Amount Per Serving
Calories 22
Calories from Fat 21
% Daily Value*
Total Fat 2.4g
4%
Cholesterol 0mg
0%
Sodium 0mg
0%
Potassium 8mg
0%
Total Carbohydrates 0.5g
0%
Protein 0.1g

Vitamin A 0%	•	Vitamin C 0%
Calcium 0%	•	Iron 1%

Nutrition Grade C-
* Based on a 2000 calorie diet

Ingredients:
- 2 cups chopped roasted turkey
- 1 teaspoon minced garlic
- 1 teaspoon ginger powder
- 1 teaspoon minced rosemary
- ½ teaspoon black pepper powder
- 3 teaspoons olive oil

Instructions:
1. Place chopped roasted turkey, minced garlic, ginger powder, minced rosemary, and black pepper powder in a food processor.
2. Process until well combined then form the mixture into small patty shape—about 10 patties.
3. Preheat a saucepan and pour olive oil into the saucepan.
4. Once it is hot, arrange the patties on the saucepan and cook for a few minutes.
5. Flip the patties and make sure the both sides are lightly brown.
6. Transfer the cooked patties on a serving dish and enjoy warm.

LUNCH: Red and Green Paleo Salads

Serving: 3

Nutrition Facts
Serving Size 124 g

Amount Per Serving

Calories 103

Calories from Fat 86

% Daily Value*

Total Fat 9.6g

15%

Saturated Fat 1.4g

7%

Trans Fat 0.0g

Cholesterol 0mg

0%

Sodium 3mg

0%

Potassium 186mg

5%

Total Carbohydrates 5.0g

2%

Dietary Fiber 1.2g

5%

Sugars 1.8g

Protein 0.9g

Vitamin A 5%   •
Calcium 4%   •

Vitamin C 7%
Iron 6%

Nutrition Grade C+

Ingredients:
- 1 teaspoon minced garlic
- 3 teaspoons sliced basil
- 3 teaspoons chopped oregano
- 1 medium cucumber
- 2 tablespoons chopped red tomato
- 2 tablespoons balsamic vinegar
- 2 tablespoons olive oil
- 1 teaspoon black pepper powder

Instructions:
- Cut the cucumber into cubes and discard the seeds. Set aside.
- Toss the cubed cucumber, tomato, minced garlic, sliced basil, and chopped oregano in a salad bowl.
- Drizzle balsamic vinegar and olive oil over the vegetable mixture then sprinkle black pepper powder on top.
- Serve and enjoy.

DINNER: Delicious Pork in Blanket

Serving: 1

Nutrition Facts
Serving Size 0 g

Amount Per Serving
Calories 0
Calories from Fat 0
% Daily Value*
Total Fat 0.0g
0%
Cholesterol 0mg
0%
Sodium 0mg
0%
Potassium 0mg
0%
Total Carbohydrates 0.0g
0%
Protein 0.0g

Vitamin A 0%	•	Vitamin C 0%
Calcium 0%	•	Iron 0%

Nutrition Grade C+
* Based on a 2000 calorie diet

Ingredients:
- 1 lb. pork meat without fat
- 2 cups homemade barbecue sauce
- 12 slices bacon
- Fresh chopped lettuce, chopped cabbage, and lemon slices for garnish

Instructions:
- Cut the pork into 6 medium cubes then place in a bowl with a lid.
- Pour barbecue sauce over the cubed pork and marinate for at least 8 hours or overnight.
- Place two slices of bacon on a flat surface then put a cube of pork on the top of the bacon.
- Carefully wrap the pork with bacon then secure with a toothpicks.
- Repeat with the remaining ingredients.
- Preheat a grill over medium heat.
- Once it is hot, grill the wrapped pork then flips until the pork is no longer pink and completely cooked.
- Arrange the grilled pork on a serving dish and serve with fresh cabbage, lettuce, and lemon slice.
- Enjoy right away.

Day 12

BREAKFAST: Tasty Pork Meatballs in Tomato Sauce

Serving: 6

Nutrition Facts
Serving Size 28 g

Amount Per Serving
Calories 15
Calories from Fat 7
% Daily Value*
Total Fat 0.8g
1%
Trans Fat 0.0g
Cholesterol 0mg
0%
Sodium 6mg
0%
Potassium 29mg
1%
Total Carbohydrates 1.2g
0%
Sugars 0.5g
Protein 0.8g

Vitamin A 0%	•	Vitamin C 1%
Calcium 0%	•	Iron 0%

Nutrition Grade B+
* Based on a 2000 calorie diet

Ingredients:
- 1 ½ cups chopped pork
- 1 organic egg white
- ½ cup chopped onion
- 3 teaspoons coconut flour
- 1 teaspoon olive oil
- ¾ teaspoon ginger powder
- 1 cup mashed tomato
- 4 tablespoons water
- 2 teaspoons apple cider vinegar
- ¼ teaspoon garlic powder

Instructions:
- First, make the sauce by combining mashed tomato, water, apple cider vinegar, garlic powder, and ¼ teaspoon ginger powder in a pot then bring to a simmer. Set aside.
- Next, preheat an oven to 350 °F and line a baking pan with parchment paper. Set aside.
- Meanwhile, place the chopped pork, egg white, onion, coconut flour, olive oil, and ginger powder together with ginger powder in a food processor.
- Process until well combined and shape into small meatballs.
- Arrange the meatballs on the prepared baking pan and bake for approximately 12 minutes.
- Transfer the baked meatballs to a serving dish then pour sauce over the meatballs.
- Serve and enjoy immediately.

LUNCH: Energetic Veggie Tuna Salads

30 DAY PALEO CHALLENGE

Servings: 4

Nutrition Facts
Serving Size 11 g

Amount Per Serving
Calories 3
Calories from Fat 0
% Daily Value*
Total Fat 0.0g
0%
Trans Fat 0.0g
Cholesterol 0mg
0%
Sodium 7mg
0%
Potassium 40mg
1%
Total Carbohydrates 0.7g
0%
Protein 0.2g

Vitamin A 7%	•	Vitamin C 9%
Calcium 1%	•	Iron 1%

Nutrition Grade A

* Based on a 2000 calorie diet

Ingredients:
- ¼ cup cooked tuna chunks
- ¼ cup chopped celery
- ¼ cup chopped parsley
- 1 teaspoon minced garlic
- ½ teaspoon black pepper powder

Instructions:
- Place all ingredients in a salad bowl.
- Using a fork mix all ingredients until combined.
- Cover the salad bowl with a lid then chill in the refrigerator for at least an hour or more.
- Enjoy cold.

DINNER: Original Steamed Broccoli

30 DAY PALEO CHALLENGE

Serving: 1

Nutrition Facts
Serving Size 142 g

Amount Per Serving
Calories 325
Calories from Fat 232
% Daily Value*
Total Fat 25.7g
40%
Saturated Fat 2.2g
11%
Trans Fat 0.0g
Cholesterol 0mg
0%
Sodium 31mg
1%
Potassium 655mg
19%
Total Carbohydrates 16.3g
5%
Dietary Fiber 6.3g
25%
Sugars 2.6g
Protein 12.8g

Vitamin A 11%	•	Vitamin C 137%
Calcium 18%	•	Iron 14%

Nutrition Grade A-
* Based on a 2000 calorie diet

Ingredients:
- 1 cup broccoli florets
- 1 teaspoon minced garlic
- 4 tablespoons chopped almonds
- 1 ½ tablespoons almond butter

Instructions:
- Pour water in a small saucepan and bring to boil.
- Once it is boiled, toss in the broccoli and cook for a few seconds. Drain and place in a bowl.
- Preheat the saucepan over medium heat then stir in almond butter, minced garlic, and chopped almonds.
- Sauté them well until the almond butter melts and the garlic is lightly golden brown.
- Drizzle almond butter on the top of the broccoli and serve right away.

Day 13

BREAKFAST: Paleo Crunchy Cereal

30 DAY PALEO CHALLENGE

Serving: 5

Nutrition Facts
Serving Size 3 g

Amount Per Serving
Calories 10
Calories from Fat 9
% Daily Value*
Total Fat 1.0g
1%
Saturated Fat 0.6g
3%
Cholesterol 0mg
0%
Sodium 0mg
0%
Potassium 11mg
0%
Total Carbohydrates 0.4g
0%
Protein 0.2g

Vitamin A 0%   Vitamin C 0%
Calcium 0%   Iron 2%
Nutrition Grade B+
* Based on a 2000 calorie diet
Nutrition Facts

124

Ingredients:
- 2 tablespoons shredded coconut
- 1 tablespoon sunflower seeds
- 1 ½ teaspoons chia seeds
- 1 teaspoon cinnamon powder
- 1 small egg white

Instructions:
- Preheat an oven to 325 °F and line a baking pan with parchment paper.
- Combine all ingredients in a food processor then process until well combined and become dough.
- Place the dough on a flat surface then roll until you have a rectangle with 1/4 –inch thick.
- Cut the dough into 1/2 –inch x 1/2 –inch squares then arranges them on the prepared baking pan.
- Bake for approximately 25 minutes until the squares are lightly brown.
- Transfer to a serving bowl and enjoy.

LUNCH: Sweet Cashew Paleo Brownie

30 DAY PALEO CHALLENGE

Serving: 4

Nutrition Facts
Serving Size 50 g

Amount Per Serving
Calories 265
Calories from Fat 201
% Daily Value*
Total Fat 22.3g
34%
Saturated Fat 4.1g
20%
Trans Fat 0.0g
Cholesterol 0mg
0%
Sodium 4mg
0%
Potassium 224mg
6%
Total Carbohydrates 16.2g
5%
Dietary Fiber 2.2g
9%
Sugars 9.0g
Protein 4.2g

Vitamin A 0%	•	Vitamin C 0%
Calcium 3%	•	Iron 8%

Nutrition Grade C+
* Based on a 2000 calorie diet

Ingredients:
- ½ cup chopped roasted cashew
- ¼ cup chopped dates
- 3 teaspoons olive oil
- ½ teaspoon raw cacao powder
- ¼ cup sliced roasted almond
- 2 tablespoons olive oil
- ½ teaspoons raw honey
- 3 teaspoons coconut milk

Instructions:
- Prepare a square tin and line with parchment paper.
- Combine half of the roasted cashew together with chopped dates, 3 teaspoons of olive oil, raw cacao powder, and roasted almond in a food processor. Pulse until the mixture is well combined.
- Pour the mixture into the prepared tin and spread evenly.
- Chill the brownie in the refrigerator for 30 minutes.
- Meanwhile, pour water in a pan then bring to boil.
- Once it is boiled, reduce the heat then place a saucepan on the boiled water.
- Pour 2 tablespoons olive oil, raw honey, and coconut milk into the saucepan. Stir well.
- Add the raw cacao powder into the saucepan and stir until incorporated. Turn the stove off and let the sauce cool.
- Remove the brownie from the refrigerator then pour chocolate sauce over the top. Spread evenly.
- Sprinkle the remaining roasted cashew on the top then return to the refrigerator for at least 3 hours or more.
- When the brownie is already set, slice and keep in the refrigerator. Enjoy.

DINNER: Tasteful Savory Shrimp Stew

Serving: 1

Nutrition Facts
Serving Size 384 g

Amount Per Serving
Calories 166
Calories from Fat 132
% Daily Value*
Total Fat 14.7g
23%
Saturated Fat 2.5g
13%
Cholesterol 0mg
0%
Sodium 24mg
1%
Potassium 212mg
6%
Total Carbohydrates 8.7g
3%
Dietary Fiber 2.1g
8%
Sugars 4.0g
Protein 1.5g

| Vitamin A 9% | • | Vitamin C 66% |
| Calcium 4% | • | Iron 2% |

Nutrition Grade C+
* Based on a 2000 calorie diet

Ingredients:
- ¾ cup fresh shrimps
- 1 teaspoon grated lime zest
- 1 teaspoon grated lemon zest
- 4 tablespoons lime juice
- 4 tablespoons lemon juice
- 4 tablespoons cilantro
- 3 teaspoons olive oil
- ½ cup chopped onion
- 1 teaspoon minced garlic
- 1 teaspoon red chili flakes
- ¼ teaspoon cayenne pepper

Instructions:
- Place half of the lemon and lime zest in a bowl with a lid.
- Add cilantro and stir until incorporated.
- Put the shrimps into the mixture and marinate for approximately 30 minutes.
- Place the olive oil in a soup pot over medium heat. Once it is hot, stir in chopped onion and minced garlic into the pot and sauté until wilted and aromatic.
- Add in red chili flakes, water, and cayenne pepper into the pot then bring to a simmer.
- After that, add the marinated shrimps into the pot and cook for approximately 6 minutes.
- Transfer the shrimp stew to a serving bowl and garnish with sprigs of leaf.
- Enjoy hot.

Day 14

BREAKFAST: Smooth Coconut Carrot Pudding

Serving: 3

Nutrition Facts
Serving Size 200 g

Amount Per Serving
Calories 49
Calories from Fat 27
% Daily Value*
Total Fat 3.0g
5%
Trans Fat 0.0g
Cholesterol 0mg
0%
Sodium 30mg
1%
Potassium 159mg
5%
Total Carbohydrates 4.5g
2%
Dietary Fiber 1.1g
4%
Sugars 1.8g
Protein 1.4g

Vitamin A 123%	•	Vitamin C 4%
Calcium 3%	•	Iron 2%

Nutrition Grade A
* Based on a 2000 calorie diet

Ingredients:
- 1 cup chopped carrots
- 2 cups water
- 3 teaspoons coconut butter
- 3 teaspoons almond butter
- ¼ teaspoon cinnamon powder
- ¼ teaspoon nutmeg powder

Instructions:
- Pour water in a pan and bring to boil.
- Once it is boiled, add in the chopped carrots then cook for approximately 15 minutes until tender.
- Drain the cooked carrots and place into a food processor.
- Add the remaining ingredients into the food processor then puree until smooth and creamy.
- Transfer the mixture to a serving bowl and enjoy right away.

LUNCH: Delicious Paleo Chicken With Sweet Potato Chips

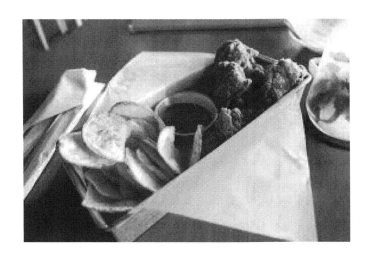

30 DAY PALEO CHALLENGE

Serving: 2

Nutrition Facts
Serving Size 210 g

Amount Per Serving
Calories 720
Calories from Fat 536
% Daily Value*
Total Fat 59.5g
92%
Saturated Fat 13.7g
69%
Cholesterol 54mg
18%
Sodium 1001mg
42%
Potassium 419mg
12%
Total Carbohydrates 29.4g
10%
Dietary Fiber 2.5g
10%
Sugars 4.5g
Protein 21.6g

Vitamin A 8%	•	Vitamin C 32%
Calcium 2%	•	Iron 18%

Nutrition Grade C
* Based on a 2000 calorie diet

Ingredients:
POTATO CHIPS
- 1 medium sweet potato
- 3 teaspoons olive oil
- 1 teaspoon chopped rosemary
- ½ teaspoon sea salt

CRISPY CHICKEN
- 1 cup chopped chicken
- 4 tablespoons tapioca starch
- ½ teaspoon sea salt
- ¼ teaspoon black pepper powder
- ¼ teaspoon paprika
- ¼ teaspoon garlic powder
- ½ cup olive oil

Instructions:
- Preheat an oven to 375 °F. Prepare a baking pan then line with parchment paper. Set aside.
- Peel the sweet potato and slice thinly using a very sharp knife.
- Season the sliced sweet potato with olive oil, chopped rosemary, and sea salt.
- Arrange the sweet potato on the prepared baking pan then bake for about 10 minutes.
- Flip each sliced potato and return to the oven for another 10 minutes. The sweet potato chips will look golden brown.
- Transfer the sweet potato chips to a bowl then set aside.
- Reduce the oven to 350 °F. Prepare another baking pan and line with parchment paper. Set aside.
- Combine tapioca starch, sea salt, black pepper powder,

paprika, and garlic powder in bowl. Stir well.
- Coat the chicken with the mixture then refrigerate for approximately 15 minutes.
- Preheat a skillet then pour olive oil into the skillet.
- Once it is hot, fry the coated chicken for about 3 minutes.
- Flip the chicken and fry for another 3 minutes until both sides of the chicken are golden brown.
- Transfer the fried chicken on the prepared baking pan and bake for about 20 minutes.
- Arrange the baked chicken and potato chips in a lunch box and enjoy at lunch.

DINNER: Scrumptious Spicy Paleo Pork Ribs

30 DAY PALEO CHALLENGE

Serving: 1

Nutrition Facts
Serving Size 148 g

Amount Per Serving
Calories 901
Calories from Fat 901
% Daily Value*
Total Fat 101.7g
156%
Saturated Fat 14.6g
73%
Cholesterol 0mg
0%
Sodium 29mg
1%
Potassium 185mg
5%
Total Carbohydrates 7.7g
3%
Dietary Fiber 3.1g
12%
Sugars 1.7g
Protein 1.4g

Vitamin A 40%	•	Vitamin C 13%
Calcium 5%	•	Iron 9%

Nutrition Grade D+

Ingredients:
- 2 lb. pork rib without fat
- ½ tablespoon minced garlic
- ¼ cup chopped onion
- 1 teaspoon paprika
- 1 teaspoon coriander
- 1 teaspoon oregano
- 1 teaspoon red chili powder
- ½ cup olive oil
- ½ teaspoon cinnamon powder
- Lemon slices, for garnish

Instructions:
- Combine minced garlic, chopped onion, paprika, coriander, oregano, and red chili powder in a bowl. Stir until incorporated.
- Rub the pork rib with the mixture and marinate for approximately 30 minutes.
- Preheat an oven to 300 °F and prepare a baking pan.
- Wrap the marinated pork rib with aluminum foil then place on the baking pan and bake for 60 minutes.
- Meanwhile, combine the olive oil with cinnamon powder, set aside.
- Remove the cooked pork rib from the oven and discard the aluminum foil.
- Grease the cooked pork with applesauce mixture then return into the oven and bake for another 30 minutes.
- Once it is done, remove from the oven then transfer to a serving dish.
- Garnish with lemon slices then serve hot.

Day 15

BREAKFAST: The Nutritious Spinach Omelet

Serving: 4

Nutrition Facts
Serving Size 43 g

Amount Per Serving
Calories 47
Calories from Fat 32
% Daily Value*
Total Fat 3.6g
5%
Saturated Fat 0.5g
3%
Trans Fat 0.0g
Cholesterol 0mg
0%
Sodium 23mg
1%
Potassium 93mg
3%
Total Carbohydrates 2.0g
1%
Sugars 0.8g
Protein 2.2g

Vitamin A 14%	•	Vitamin C 6%
Calcium 1%	•	Iron 1%

Nutrition Grade B
* Based on a 2000 calorie diet

Ingredients:
- 1 tablespoon olive oil
- ½ cup chopped onion
- 1 teaspoon minced garlic
- 1 cup chopped spinach
- 2 organic egg whites
- ¼ teaspoon black pepper powder

Instructions:
- Preheat a skillet over medium heat then pour olive oil into the skillet.
- Once it is hot, stir in chopped onion and dice garlic into the skillet then sauté until wilted and lightly golden brown. Set aside.
- Place the egg whites and beat them in a medium bowl. After that, put the sautéed onion and garlic then add the remaining ingredients into the beaten eggs.
- Preheat an oven to 350 °°F and line a baking pan with parchment paper.
- Pour the egg mixture into the prepared baking pan and bake for approximately 15 minutes until lightly brown.
- Transfer the baked omelet to a serving dish then serve immediately.
- Best to be enjoyed with tomato sauce.

LUNCH: Simple Tomato Red Soup

30 DAY PALEO CHALLENGE

Serving: 3

Nutrition Facts
Serving Size 14 g

Amount Per Serving
Calories 20
Calories from Fat 14
% Daily Value*
Total Fat 1.6g
2%
Cholesterol 0mg
0%
Sodium 3mg
0%
Potassium 38mg
1%
Total Carbohydrates 1.6g
1%
Sugars 0.6g
Protein 0.3g

Vitamin A 1%   •   Vitamin C 3%
Calcium 1%   •   Iron 1%
Nutrition Grade B
* Based on a 2000 calorie diet

Ingredients:
- 2 medium red tomatoes
- ¼ cup chopped onion
- 1 teaspoon minced garlic
- 1 teaspoon olive oil
- 1 teaspoon chopped parsley
- ¾ cup vegetable stock
- 1 teaspoon tomato paste
- ¼ teaspoon pepper powder

Instructions:
- Preheat an oven to 350 °F. Prepare a baking pan and line with parchment paper. Set aside.
- Cut the red tomatoes into wedges then arrange on the prepared baking pan.
- Place onion and minced garlic among the tomatoes then splash olive oil over the tomatoes and onion.
- Sprinkle pepper and chopped parsley on the top then bake for approximately 40 minutes. The tomatoes will reduce for approximately half their size.
- Remove the baked ingredients from the oven and set aside.
- Combine vegetable stock with tomato paste in a pan then bring to boil.
- Add the baked ingredients into the vegetable stock and bring to a simmer for approximately 10 minutes.
- Let it stand for a few minutes and when it is warm, transfer the mixture to a blender.
- Blend until smooth and incorporated and pour into a serving bowl.
- Garnish with fresh parsley on top then serve warm.

DINNER: Original Beef Patties with Scrumptious Sauce

30 DAY PALEO CHALLENGE

Serving: 1

Nutrition Facts
Serving Size 552 g

Amount Per Serving
Calories 1,905
Calories from Fat 1905
% Daily Value*
Total Fat 211.7g
326%
Saturated Fat 30.4g
152%
Trans Fat 0.0g
Cholesterol 0mg
0%
Sodium 71mg
3%
Potassium 594mg
17%
Total Carbohydrates 20.4g
7%
Dietary Fiber 5.2g
21%
Sugars 8.4g
Protein 4.5g

Vitamin A 7%	•	Vitamin C 24%
Calcium 19%	•	Iron 19%

Nutrition Grade D

Ingredients:

PATTIES
- ¼ cup chopped onion
- 1 teaspoon olive oil
- 1 cup minced beef
- ¼ cup grated beetroot
- 1 teaspoon diced garlic
- 1 tablespoon chopped rosemary
- 1 teaspoon black pepper powder
- 1 cup olive oil, for frying
- 1 cup sliced cucumber

CUCUMBER SALADS
- 1 cup sliced cucumber
- 1 teaspoon lemon zest
- 3 teaspoons sesame seeds
- 2 tablespoons apple cider vinegar
- ½ teaspoon Dijon mustard
- ¼ teaspoon black pepper powder

GARNISH
- Fresh lettuce
- Fresh parsley

Instructions:
- Preheat a skillet then pour olive oil into the skillet.
- Once it is hot, stir in onion and sauté until wilted and aromatic.
- Place the sautéed onion together with the patties ingredients in a bowl and mix well.
- Using your hands, mold the mixture into small patties.
- Preheat a frying pan then pour a cup of olive oil into the pan.

- Once it is hot, arrange the patties on the pan and cook for approximately 6 minutes.
- Carefully flip the patties and cook another side for 6 minutes as well—the beetroot can easily burn so avoid high heat in frying the patties.
- Once the patties are cooked, remove from the pan and let them cool for a few minutes.
- Meanwhile, combine the salad ingredients in a bowl and mix until incorporated.
- Arrange fresh lettuce on a serving dish then put the patties on the lettuce.
- Drizzle sauce over the patties and garnish with fresh parsley.
- Serve and enjoy at dinner.

Day 16

BREAKFAST: Delicious Coconut Pancake with Strawberry Sauce

30 DAY PALEO CHALLENGE

Serving: 6

Nutrition Facts
Serving Size 21 g

Amount Per Serving
Calories 24
Calories from Fat 21
% Daily Value*
Total Fat 2.4g
4%
Trans Fat 0.0g
Cholesterol 0mg
0%
Sodium 1mg
0%
Potassium 61mg
2%
Total Carbohydrates 1.1g
0%
Sugars 0.6g
Protein 0.1g

Vitamin A 0%	•	Vitamin C 12%
Calcium 2%	•	Iron 0%

Nutrition Grade C+
* Based on a 2000 calorie diet

153

Ingredients:
- ¼ cup coconut flour
- 4 fresh organic eggs white
- 2 ½ tablespoons water
- 3 teaspoons olive oil
- ½ teaspoon baking powder
- ¼ teaspoon apple cider vinegar
- ½ cup fresh strawberries
- Fresh strawberries, for garnish

Instructions:
- Combine coconut flour and eggs whites in a bowl.
- Using a hand mixer beat them until smooth and creamy then adds water and olive oil into the mixture.
- Meanwhile, preheat a saucepan over low heat.
- Stir in baking powder and apple cider vinegar a few seconds before pouring the mixture into the hot saucepan.
- Take about ¼ cup of the mixture and pour into the hot saucepan. Cook for approximately 30 seconds then flip the pancake.
- Make sure that both sides of the pancake are lightly golden brown.
- Repeat to the remaining mixture and set aside.
- After that, place fresh strawberries in a blender then blend on high speed until creamy and incorporated.
- Put a pancake on a serving dish and coat with strawberry sauce.
- Cover with another pancake and repeat with the remaining pancakes and strawberry sauce.
- Garnish with fresh strawberries and serve immediately.

LUNCH: Nutritious Mixed Salads

Serving: 3

Nutrition Facts
Serving Size 66 g

Amount Per Serving
Calories 31
Calories from Fat 2
% Daily Value*
Total Fat 0.2g
0%
Trans Fat 0.0g
Cholesterol 0mg
0%
Sodium 165mg
7%
Potassium 122mg
3%
Total Carbohydrates 7.7g
3%
Dietary Fiber 1.0g
4%
Sugars 5.5g
Protein 0.6g

Vitamin A 19%	•	Vitamin C 49%
Calcium 2%	•	Iron 4%

Nutrition Grade A
* Based on a 2000 calorie diet

Ingredients:
- 1 cup chopped spinach
- 1 cup shredded sea bass
- 1 cup chopped pineapple
- ½ cup chopped half ripe papaya
- ½ teaspoon cumin
- ¼ teaspoon black pepper powder

Instructions:
- Steam the bass until cooked then set aside.
- Layer spinach, pineapple, papaya, and steamed sea bass in a salad bowl.
- Season with cumin and pepper then serve right away.

DINNER: Spiced Beef Stew with Carrots and Blueberries

Serving: 3

Nutrition Facts
Serving Size 96 g

Amount Per Serving

Calories 152

Calories from Fat 112

% Daily Value*

Total Fat 12.4g

19%

Saturated Fat 1.6g

8%

Trans Fat 0.0g

Cholesterol 0mg

0%

Sodium 182mg

8%

Potassium 209mg

6%

Total Carbohydrates 10.1g

3%

Dietary Fiber 2.2g

9%

Sugars 5.1g

Protein 1.9g

| Vitamin A 123% | • | Vitamin C 12% |
| Calcium 3% | • | Iron 4% |

Nutrition Grade B+

* Based on a 2000 calorie diet

Ingredients:
- 2 cups chopped beef
- ½ cup fresh blueberries
- 1 cup chopped carrots
- 1 tablespoon almond butter
- 2 tablespoons olive oil
- ¼ teaspoon sea salt
- ¼ teaspoon black pepper
- ¼ teaspoon garlic powder
- ½ cup sliced onion

Instructions:
- Preheat a skillet then pour olive oil into the skillet.
- Once it is hot, stir in chopped beef and onion then sauté until the onion is aromatic and the beef is wilted.
- Season the beef with sea salt, black pepper powder, and garlic powder.
- Add the chopped carrots and cook stir until cooked.
- Last, add in the blueberries and butter then stir until the butter melts.
- Transfer the cooked beef to a serving dish and serve warm.

Day 17

BREAKFAST: Scrumptious Macadamia Paleo Waffles

30 DAY PALEO CHALLENGE

Serving: 5

Nutrition Facts

Serving Size 23 g

Amount Per Serving

Calories 56

Calories from Fat 52

% Daily Value*

Total Fat 5.8g

9%

Saturated Fat 0.9g

4%

Cholesterol 0mg

0%

Sodium 58mg

2%

Potassium 30mg

1%

Total Carbohydrates 0.8g

0%

Protein 1.0g

Vitamin A 0%	•	Vitamin C 0%
Calcium 1%	•	Iron 1%

Nutrition Grade C+

* Based on a 2000 calorie diet

Nutrition Facts

Serving Size 23 g

Ingredients:
- 1 organic egg white
- 4 tablespoons chopped macadamia nuts
- 2 teaspoons olive oil
- 3 teaspoons coconut flour
- ¼ teaspoon baking soda
- ¼ cup water

Instructions:

- Place all of the ingredients in a bowl. Using a hand mixer beat until smooth and incorporated.
- Preheat a waffle iron over low heat then pour the mixture into the hot waffle iron.
- Cook for approximately 45 minutes then transfer the waffles to a serving dish..
- Best to be served with unsweetened fruit juice as healthy breakfast.

LUNCH: Jalapeno Chicken in Lettuce Tacos

30 DAY PALEO CHALLENGE

Serving: 4

Nutrition Facts
Serving Size 104 g

Amount Per Serving
Calories 109
Calories from Fat 71
% Daily Value*
Total Fat 7.9g
12%
Saturated Fat 1.0g
5%
Trans Fat 0.0g
Cholesterol 16mg
5%
Sodium 143mg
6%
Potassium 227mg
6%
Total Carbohydrates 3.9g
1%
Dietary Fiber 1.0g
4%
Sugars 2.3g
Protein 6.8g

Vitamin A 12%	•	Vitamin C 17%
Calcium 1%	•	Iron 4%

Nutrition Grade B+
* Based on a 2000 calorie diet

Ingredients:
- ½ cup chicken strips
- 2 tablespoons olive oil
- ¼ cup chopped onion
- 1 ½ cup chopped tomatoes
- 1 tablespoon jalapeno chili
- ½ teaspoon cumin
- ¼ teaspoon brown sugar
- ¼ teaspoon sea salt
- ¼ teaspoon pepper powder
- Fresh lettuce leaves, for the tacos
- 1 tablespoon chopped leek
- 1 tablespoon sliced jalapeno chilies

Instructions:
- Preheat a skillet then pour olive oil into the skillet.
- Once it is hot, stir in chicken strips and fry until golden brown. Set aside.
- In the same skillet, sauté the chopped onion until wilted and aromatic then add chopped tomatoes, jalapeno chilies, cumin, brown sugar, sea salt, and pepper powder. Bring to a simmer for approximately 15 minutes until the mixture is thicken.
- Return the chicken into the sauce and cook for another 5 minutes.
- Prepare a fresh lettuce on a flat surface then put a scoop of cooked chicken and sauce on the lettuce.
- Sprinkle chopped leek and sliced jalapeno chili then carefully wrap with the lettuce.
- Repeat to the remaining lettuce and chicken and arrange on a serving dish.
- Serve and enjoy.

166

DINNER: Grilled Chicken Spicy

Servings: 2

Nutrition Facts

Serving Size 350 g

Amount Per Serving

Calories 1,286

Calories from Fat 1018

% Daily Value*

Total Fat 113.1g

174%

Saturated Fat 15.0g

75%

Trans Fat 0.0g

Cholesterol 194mg

65%

Sodium 981mg

41%

Potassium 719mg

21%

Total Carbohydrates 4.0g

1%

Dietary Fiber 2.0g

8%

Sugars 0.8g

Protein 73.8g

Vitamin A 45%	•	Vitamin C 8%
Calcium 5%	•	Iron 23%

Nutrition Grade C+

* Based on a 2000 calorie diet

Ingredients:
- 1 lb. chicken breast
- 1 cup olive oil, to fry
- 1 tablespoon sweet paprika
- 1 teaspoon chili powder
- ¾ teaspoon sea salt
- ½ teaspoon allspice
- 1 teaspoon black pepper powder
- 1 ½ teaspoon olive oil
- 1 teaspoon minced garlic
- 1 teaspoon tomato paste
- 1 tablespoon lime juice
- Lemon slices, for garnish

Instructions:
- Cut the chicken breast into slices. Set aside.
- Place sweet paprika, chili powder, sea salt, allspice, black pepper powder, olive oil, minced garlic, tomato paste, and lime juice in a bowl. Stir well.
- Add the chicken into the mixture and marinate for at least 30 minutes.
- Preheat a grill over medium heat. Once it is hot, cook the chicken for approximately 4 minutes then flips it. Make sure that both sides of the chicken are golden brown.
- Remove the chicken from the grill and transfer to a serving dish.
- Garnish with lemon slices and enjoy.

Day 18

BREAKFAST: Delectable Ginger Banana Paleo Bars

Serving: 8

Nutrition Facts
Serving Size 20 g

Amount Per Serving
Calories 52
Calories from Fat 39
% Daily Value*
Total Fat 4.3g
7%
Cholesterol 0mg
0%
Sodium 80mg
3%
Potassium 57mg
2%
Total Carbohydrates 3.6g
1%
Sugars 1.8g
Protein 0.2g

Vitamin A 0%   •   Vitamin C 2%
Calcium 0%   •   Iron 0%
Nutrition Grade C+
* Based on a 2000 calorie diet

Nutrition Facts
Serving Size 20 g

Ingredients:
- 1 medium ripe banana
- ½ cup almond flour
- 2 ½ tablespoons almond oil
- 3 organic eggs whites
- ¾ teaspoon ginger powder
- 1 teaspoon cinnamon powder
- ½ teaspoon cardamom
- ½ teaspoon baking soda

Instructions:
- Preheat an oven to 350 °F and line a small baking pan with parchment paper.
- Peel the banana and cut into slices.
- Place the sliced banana in a food processor together with almond oil, eggs whites, ginger powder, cinnamon powder, and cardamom. Process until smooth and incorporated.
- Add in the baking soda then quickly stir until well combined.
- Pour the mixture into the prepared baking pan and bake for approximately 30 minutes.
- Once it is done, remove from the oven and let it cool for about 30 minutes.
- Cut into bars and arrange on a serving dish.
- Serve and enjoy.

LUNCH: Paleo Salads in Jar

30 DAY PALEO CHALLENGE

Serving: 2

Nutrition Facts
Serving Size 144 g

Amount Per Serving
Calories 100
Calories from Fat 45
% Daily Value*
Total Fat 5.0g
8%
Saturated Fat 0.9g
4%
Trans Fat 0.0g
Cholesterol 16mg
5%
Sodium 135mg
6%
Potassium 329mg
9%
Total Carbohydrates 8.2g
3%
Dietary Fiber 2.1g
9%
Sugars 4.0g
Protein 6.3g

| Vitamin A 112% | • | Vitamin C 60% |
| Calcium 3% | • | Iron 7% |

Nutrition Grade A
* Based on a 2000 calorie diet

Ingredients:
- 1 ½ teaspoons olive oil
- ¼ cup chopped chicken fillet
- ½ cup sliced carrots
- ½ cup sliced bell pepper
- ¼ cup chopped onion
- 1 teaspoon minced garlic
- ¼ cup mashed avocado
- 1 tablespoon lime juice
- 2 tablespoons salsa
- 2 tablespoons chopped tomato
- ½ cup cubed cucumber
- ¼ cup chopped cilantro
- 1 cup chopped fresh lettuce

Instructions
- Preheat a skillet then pour half of the olive oil into the skillet.
- Once it is hot, stir in chopped chicken fillet and cook until golden brown.
- Set aside.
- In the same skillet, pour the remaining olive oil then cooks the sliced carrot until tender.
- Add the sliced bell pepper, onion, and garlic then sauté for a few minutes. Turn the stove off.
- Combine mashed avocado and lime juice until incorporated then set aside.
- Place salsa in the bottom of the jar and spread evenly.
- Layer with avocado mixture, continued with cooked vegetables, then put chicken over the vegetables.
- Add chopped tomato and cucumber then place cilantro

and fresh lettuce on top.
- Cover the jar with the lid then refrigerate until you want to consume it.
- Enjoy!

DINNER: Spicy Beef and Butternut Squash Stew

30 DAY PALEO CHALLENGE

Serving: 1

Nutrition Facts
Serving Size 606 g

Amount Per Serving

Calories 182
Calories from Fat 129

% Daily Value*

Total Fat 14.4g
22%
Saturated Fat 2.1g
11%
Trans Fat 0.0g
Cholesterol 0mg
0%
Sodium 93mg
4%
Potassium 437mg
12%
Total Carbohydrates 14.5g
5%
Dietary Fiber 4.2g
17%
Sugars 6.5g
Protein 1.5g

Vitamin A 387%	•	Vitamin C 15%
Calcium 8%	•	Iron 6%

Nutrition Grade B+
* Based on a 2000 calorie diet

Ingredients:
- 1 tablespoon olive oil
- 2 cups cubed beef
- 1 teaspoon minced garlic
- 2 teaspoons minced sage
- ¼ teaspoon smoked paprika
- 1 tablespoon chopped red chilies
- 2 cups cubed butternut squash
- 1 cup chopped carrots
- 2 cups water
- ¼ teaspoon pepper powder

Instructions:
- Preheat olive oil in a Dutch oven over medium heat. Once it is hot, brown the cubed beef until half cooked and wilted. Set aside.
- Toss the minced garlic, sage, chopped red chilies and smoked paprika in the skillet then season with pepper powder.
- Return the cooked beef into the skillet together with cubed butternut squash and carrots then pour water over the beef.
- Bring to boil then reduce the heat and cook for an hour or more until the beef is tender.
- Transfer the stew to a serving bowl then enjoy hot.

Day 19

BREAKFAST: Spicy Vegetable Casserole

30 DAY PALEO CHALLENGE

Serving: 6

Nutrition Facts
Serving Size 27 g

Amount Per Serving

Calories 16

Calories from Fat 7

% Daily Value*

Total Fat 0.8g

1%

Trans Fat 0.0g

Cholesterol 0mg

0%

Sodium 17mg

1%

Potassium 71mg

2%

Total Carbohydrates 1.9g

1%

Dietary Fiber 0.6g

2%

Sugars 0.6g

Protein 0.5g

Vitamin A 16% • Vitamin C 18%
Calcium 1% • Iron 2%
Nutrition Grade A

* Based on a 2000 calorie diet

Nutrition Facts

Ingredients:
- 1 cup chopped spinach
- ½ cup broccoli florets
- 1 teaspoon olive oil
- ½ cup chopped onion
- 1 tablespoon chopped green chili
- 1 teaspoon minced garlic
- 2 organic eggs whites, lightly beaten
- ¼ teaspoon black pepper powder
- 1 tablespoon chopped parsley, for garnish

Instructions:
- Preheat an oven to 375 °F and grease a small casserole dish with cooking spray.
- Preheat a skillet then pour olive oil into the skillet.
- Once it is hot, stir in chopped onion, minced garlic and green chilies into the skillet and sauté until wilted and aromatic.
- Transfer the sautéed onion mixture to the beaten eggs then season with black pepper powder.
- Add the chopped spinach and broccoli florets into the egg mixture and stir well.
- Pour the mixture into the prepared casserole dish then bake for approximately 45 minutes.
- Once it is cooked, remove the casserole from the oven and let it cool for about five minutes.
- Sprinkle chopped parsley on the top for garnish.
- Serve and enjoy warm.

LUNCH: Red and Green Paleo Salads

Serving: 3

Nutrition Facts
Serving Size 124 g

Amount Per Serving
Calories 103
Calories from Fat 86
% Daily Value*
Total Fat 9.6g
15%
Saturated Fat 1.4g
7%
Trans Fat 0.0g
Cholesterol 0mg
0%
Sodium 3mg
0%
Potassium 186mg
5%
Total Carbohydrates 5.0g
2%
Dietary Fiber 1.2g
5%
Sugars 1.8g
Protein 0.9g

| Vitamin A 5% | • | Vitamin C 7% |
| Calcium 4% | • | Iron 6% |

Nutrition Grade C+

Ingredients:
- 1 teaspoon minced garlic
- 3 teaspoons sliced basil
- 3 teaspoons chopped oregano
- 1 medium cucumber
- 2 tablespoons chopped red tomato
- 2 tablespoons balsamic vinegar
- 2 tablespoons olive oil
- 1 teaspoon black pepper powder

Instructions:
- Cut the cucumber into cubes and discard the seeds. Set aside.
- Toss the cubed cucumber, tomato, minced garlic, sliced basil, and chopped oregano in a salad bowl.
- Drizzle balsamic vinegar and olive oil over the vegetable mixture then sprinkle black pepper powder on top.
- Serve and enjoy.

DINNER: Delicious Simple Baked Salmon

Serving: 2

Nutrition Facts
Serving Size 244 g

Amount Per Serving
Calories 365
Calories from Fat 190
% Daily Value*
Total Fat 21.1g
33%
Saturated Fat 3.1g
15%
Trans Fat 0.0g
Cholesterol 100mg
33%
Sodium 336mg
14%
Potassium 889mg
25%
Total Carbohydrates 0.8g
0%
Protein 44.2g

Vitamin A 5%	•	Vitamin C 7%
Calcium 10%	•	Iron 15%

Nutrition Grade C+
* Based on a 2000 calorie diet

Ingredients:

- 1 lb. salmon fillet
- 1 tablespoon lemon juice
- ¼ teaspoon sea salt
- ¼ teaspoon black pepper powder
- 2 teaspoons chopped thyme
- 1 tablespoon olive oil

Instructions:

- Preheat an oven to 400 °F then lines a baking pan with parchment paper.
- Place salmon on the prepared baking pan then season with salt and black pepper.
- Next, splash lemon juice over the salmon and sprinkle thyme on top.
- After that, drizzle with olive oil and bake for approximately 25 minutes.
- Once it is done, remove the cooked salmon from the oven then transfer to a serving dish.
- Serve immediately.

Day 20

BREAKFAST: Paleo Simple Almond Muffin

Serving: 4

Nutrition Facts
Serving Size 18 g

Amount Per Serving
Calories 65
Calories from Fat 61
% Daily Value*
Total Fat 6.8g
10%
Saturated Fat 0.6g
3%
Trans Fat 0.0g
Cholesterol 0mg
0%
Sodium 88mg
4%
Potassium 16mg
0%
Total Carbohydrates 0.3g
0%
Protein 0.9g

Vitamin A 0%   •   Vitamin C 0%
Calcium 0%   •   Iron 0%
Nutrition Grade D+
* Based on a 2000 calorie diet
Nutrition Facts

Ingredients:

- 2 tablespoons almond flour
- 2 tablespoons almond oil
- 1 organic egg white
- 1 ½ teaspoons unsweetened apple juice
- ¼ teaspoon baking soda
- ½ teaspoon apple cider vinegar
- Roasted sliced almonds, for garnish

Instructions:

- Preheat an oven to 350 °F and prepare 3 muffin paper cups.
- Place almond flour, almond oil, and egg whites in a bowl. Stir until smooth and incorporated.
- Pour unsweetened apple juice into the mixture then baking soda, and apple cider vinegar into the mixture.
- Stir until well combined then divide the mixture into 3 muffin paper cups.
- Sprinkle sliced almond on the top then bake for approximately 20 minutes or until a toothpick comes out clean.
- Remove the muffins from the oven and let them cool for about 30 minutes.
- Serve and enjoy.

LUNCH: Energetic Veggie Tuna Salads

30 DAY PALEO CHALLENGE

Servings: 4

Nutrition Facts
Serving Size 11 g

Amount Per Serving
Calories 3
Calories from Fat 0
% Daily Value*
Total Fat 0.0g
0%
Trans Fat 0.0g
Cholesterol 0mg
0%
Sodium 7mg
0%
Potassium 40mg
1%
Total Carbohydrates 0.7g
0%
Protein 0.2g

Vitamin A 7%	•	Vitamin C 9%
Calcium 1%	•	Iron 1%

Nutrition Grade A

* Based on a 2000 calorie diet

Ingredients:
- ¼ cup cooked tuna chunks
- ¼ cup chopped celery
- ¼ cup chopped parsley
- 1 teaspoon minced garlic
- ½ teaspoon black pepper powder

Instructions:
- Place all ingredients in a salad bowl.
- Using a fork mix all ingredients until combined.
- Cover the salad bowl with a lid then chill in the refrigerator for at least an hour or more.
- Enjoy cold.

DINNER: Delicious Pork in Blanket

30 DAY PALEO CHALLENGE

Serving: 1

Nutrition Facts
Serving Size 0 g

Amount Per Serving

Calories 0
Calories from Fat 0

% Daily Value*

Total Fat 0.0g
0%

Cholesterol 0mg
0%

Sodium 0mg
0%

Potassium 0mg
0%

Total Carbohydrates 0.0g
0%

Protein 0.0g

| Vitamin A 0% | • | Vitamin C 0% |
| Calcium 0% | • | Iron 0% |

Nutrition Grade C+
* Based on a 2000 calorie diet

Ingredients:
- 1 lb. pork meat without fat
- 2 cups homemade barbecue sauce
- 12 slices bacon
- Fresh chopped lettuce, chopped cabbage, and lemon slices for garnish

Instructions:
- Cut the pork into 6 medium cubes then place in a bowl with a lid.
- Pour barbecue sauce over the cubed pork and marinate for at least 8 hours or overnight.
- Place two slices of bacon on a flat surface then put a cube of pork on the top of the bacon.
- Carefully wrap the pork with bacon then secure with a toothpicks.
- Repeat with the remaining ingredients.
- Preheat a grill over medium heat.
- Once it is hot, grill the wrapped pork then flips until the pork is no longer pink and completely cooked.
- Arrange the grilled pork on a serving dish and serve with fresh cabbage, lettuce, and lemon slice.
- Enjoy right away.

Day 21

BREAKFAST: Paleo Warm Turkey Fritters

Serving: 6

Nutrition Facts
Serving Size 3 g

Amount Per Serving
Calories 22
Calories from Fat 21
% Daily Value*
Total Fat 2.4g
4%
Cholesterol 0mg
0%
Sodium 0mg
0%
Potassium 8mg
0%
Total Carbohydrates 0.5g
0%
Protein 0.1g

Vitamin A 0%	•	Vitamin C 0%
Calcium 0%	•	Iron 1%

Nutrition Grade C-
* Based on a 2000 calorie diet

Ingredients:
- 2 cups chopped roasted turkey
- 1 teaspoon minced garlic
- 1 teaspoon ginger powder
- 1 teaspoon minced rosemary
- ½ teaspoon black pepper powder
- 3 teaspoons olive oil

Instructions:
- Place chopped roasted turkey, minced garlic, ginger powder, minced rosemary, and black pepper powder in a food processor.
- Process until well combined then form the mixture into small patty shape—about 10 patties.
- Preheat a saucepan and pour olive oil into the saucepan.
- Once it is hot, arrange the patties on the saucepan and cook for a few minutes.
- Flip the patties and make sure the both sides are lightly brown.
- Transfer the cooked patties on a serving dish and enjoy warm.

LUNCH: Original Steamed Broccoli

Serving: 1

Nutrition Facts
Serving Size 142 g

Amount Per Serving
Calories 325
Calories from Fat 232
% Daily Value*
Total Fat 25.7g
40%
Saturated Fat 2.2g
11%
Trans Fat 0.0g
Cholesterol 0mg
0%
Sodium 31mg
1%
Potassium 655mg
19%
Total Carbohydrates 16.3g
5%
Dietary Fiber 6.3g
25%
Sugars 2.6g
Protein 12.8g

| Vitamin A 11% | • | Vitamin C 137% |
| Calcium 18% | • | Iron 14% |

Nutrition Grade A-
* Based on a 2000 calorie diet

Ingredients:
- 1 cup broccoli florets
- 1 teaspoon minced garlic
- 4 tablespoons chopped almonds
- 1 ½ tablespoons almond butter

Instructions:
- Pour water in a small saucepan and bring to boil.
- Once it is boiled, toss in the broccoli and cook for a few seconds. Drain and place in a bowl.
- Preheat the saucepan over medium heat then stir in almond butter, minced garlic, and chopped almonds.
- Sauté them well until the almond butter melts and the garlic is lightly golden brown.
- Drizzle almond butter on the top of the broccoli and serve right away.

DINNER: Spicy Chicken Kebab

Serving: 2

Nutrition Facts
Serving Size 40 g

Amount Per Serving
Calories 237
Calories from Fat 230
% Daily Value*
Total Fat 25.5g
39%
Saturated Fat 3.6g
18%
Trans Fat 0.0g
Cholesterol 0mg
0%
Sodium 85mg
4%
Potassium 14mg
0%
Total Carbohydrates 4.8g
2%
Sugars 4.4g
Protein 0.4g

Vitamin A 0%	•	Vitamin C 0%
Calcium 0%	•	Iron 1%

Nutrition Grade D
* Based on a 2000 calorie diet

Ingredients:
- 1 lb. boneless chicken breast without fat
- ¼ cup olive oil
- 3 teaspoons yellow mustard
- ½ tablespoon raw honey
- Lemon slices, for garnish
- Lettuce, for garnish

Instructions:
- Combine olive oil, yellow mustard, and raw honey in a bowl.
- Cut the boneless chicken into cubes.
- Skewer the cubed chicken with wooden skewers then grease with the sauce.
- Preheat a grill pan and once it is hot, grill the chicken over medium heat until completely cooked.
- Repeat to grease the chicken with sauce during the grilling process.
- Arrange the grilled chicken on a serving dish and garnish with fresh lettuce and sliced lemon.
- Serve and enjoy warm.

Day 22

BREAKFAST: Tasty Pork Meatballs in Tomato Sauce

30 DAY PALEO CHALLENGE

Serving: 6

Nutrition Facts
Serving Size 28 g

Amount Per Serving
Calories 15
Calories from Fat 7
% Daily Value*
Total Fat 0.8g
1%
Trans Fat 0.0g
Cholesterol 0mg
0%
Sodium 6mg
0%
Potassium 29mg
1%
Total Carbohydrates 1.2g
0%
Sugars 0.5g
Protein 0.8g

Vitamin A 0%	•	Vitamin C 1%
Calcium 0%	•	Iron 0%

Nutrition Grade B+
* Based on a 2000 calorie diet

Ingredients:
- 1 ½ cups chopped pork
- 1 organic egg white
- ½ cup chopped onion
- 3 teaspoons coconut flour
- 1 teaspoon olive oil
- ¾ teaspoon ginger powder
- 1 cup mashed tomato
- 4 tablespoons water
- 2 teaspoons apple cider vinegar
- ¼ teaspoon garlic powder

Instructions:
- First, make the sauce by combining mashed tomato, water, apple cider vinegar, garlic powder, and ¼ teaspoon ginger powder in a pot then bring to a simmer. Set aside.
- Next, preheat an oven to 350 °F and line a baking pan with parchment paper. Set aside.
- Meanwhile, place the chopped pork, egg white, onion, coconut flour, olive oil, and ginger powder together with ginger powder in a food processor.
- Process until well combined and shape into small meatballs.
- Arrange the meatballs on the prepared baking pan and bake for approximately 12 minutes.
- Transfer the baked meatballs to a serving dish then pour sauce over the meatballs.
- Serve and enjoy immediately.

LUNCH: Delicious Paleo Chicken With Sweet Potato Chips

30 DAY PALEO CHALLENGE

Serving: 2

Nutrition Facts

Serving Size 210 g

Amount Per Serving

Calories 720

Calories from Fat 536

% Daily Value*

Total Fat 59.5g

92%

Saturated Fat 13.7g

69%

Cholesterol 54mg

18%

Sodium 1001mg

42%

Potassium 419mg

12%

Total Carbohydrates 29.4g

10%

Dietary Fiber 2.5g

10%

Sugars 4.5g

Protein 21.6g

| Vitamin A 8% | • | Vitamin C 32% |
| Calcium 2% | • | Iron 18% |

Nutrition Grade C

* Based on a 2000 calorie diet

Ingredients:
POTATO CHIPS
- 1 medium sweet potato
- 3 teaspoons olive oil
- 1 teaspoon chopped rosemary
- ½ teaspoon sea salt

CRISPY CHICKEN
- 1 cup chopped chicken
- 4 tablespoons tapioca starch
- ½ teaspoon sea salt
- ¼ teaspoon black pepper powder
- ¼ teaspoon paprika
- ¼ teaspoon garlic powder
- ½ cup olive oil

Instructions:
- Preheat an oven to 375 °F. Prepare a baking pan then line with parchment paper. Set aside.
- Peel the sweet potato and slice thinly using a very sharp knife.
- Season the sliced sweet potato with olive oil, chopped rosemary, and sea salt.
- Arrange the sweet potato on the prepared baking pan then bake for about 10 minutes.
- Flip each sliced potato and return to the oven for another 10 minutes. The sweet potato chips will look golden brown.
- Transfer the sweet potato chips to a bowl then set aside.
- Reduce the oven to 350 °F. Prepare another baking pan and line with parchment paper. Set aside.
- Combine tapioca starch, sea salt, black pepper powder,

212

paprika, and garlic powder in bowl. Stir well.
- Coat the chicken with the mixture then refrigerate for approximately 15 minutes.
- Preheat a skillet then pour olive oil into the skillet.
- Once it is hot, fry the coated chicken for about 3 minutes.
- Flip the chicken and fry for another 3 minutes until both sides of the chicken are golden brown.
- Transfer the fried chicken on the prepared baking pan and bake for about 20 minutes.
- Arrange the baked chicken and potato chips in a lunch box and enjoy at lunch.

DINNER: Tasteful Savory Shrimp Stew

Serving: 1

Nutrition Facts

Serving Size 384 g

Amount Per Serving

Calories 166

Calories from Fat 132

% Daily Value*

Total Fat 14.7g

23%

Saturated Fat 2.5g

13%

Cholesterol 0mg

0%

Sodium 24mg

1%

Potassium 212mg

6%

Total Carbohydrates 8.7g

3%

Dietary Fiber 2.1g

8%

Sugars 4.0g

Protein 1.5g

Vitamin A 9%	•	Vitamin C 66%
Calcium 4%	•	Iron 2%

Nutrition Grade C+

* Based on a 2000 calorie diet

Ingredients:
- ¾ cup fresh shrimps
- 1 teaspoon grated lime zest
- 1 teaspoon grated lemon zest
- 4 tablespoons lime juice
- 4 tablespoons lemon juice
- 4 tablespoons cilantro
- 3 teaspoons olive oil
- ½ cup chopped onion
- 1 teaspoon minced garlic
- 1 teaspoon red chili flakes
- ¼ teaspoon cayenne pepper

Instructions:
- Place half of the lemon and lime zest in a bowl with a lid.
- Add cilantro and stir until incorporated.
- Put the shrimps into the mixture and marinate for approximately 30 minutes.
- Place the olive oil in a soup pot over medium heat. Once it is hot, stir in chopped onion and minced garlic into the pot and sauté until wilted and aromatic.
- Add in red chili flakes, water, and cayenne pepper into the pot then bring to a simmer.
- After that, add the marinated shrimps into the pot and cook for approximately 6 minutes.
- Transfer the shrimp stew to a serving bowl and garnish with sprigs of leaf.
- Enjoy hot.

Day 23

BREAKFAST: Paleo Crunchy Cereal

Serving: 5

Nutrition Facts
Serving Size 3 g

Amount Per Serving
Calories 10
Calories from Fat 9
% Daily Value*
Total Fat 1.0g
1%
Saturated Fat 0.6g
3%
Cholesterol 0mg
0%
Sodium 0mg
0%
Potassium 11mg
0%
Total Carbohydrates 0.4g
0%
Protein 0.2g

Vitamin A 0% Vitamin C 0%
Calcium 0% Iron 2%
Nutrition Grade B+
* Based on a 2000 calorie diet
Nutrition Facts

Ingredients:
- 2 tablespoons shredded coconut
- 1 tablespoon sunflower seeds
- 1 ½ teaspoons chia seeds
- 1 teaspoon cinnamon powder
- 1 small egg white

Instructions:
- Preheat an oven to 325 °F and line a baking pan with parchment paper.
- Combine all ingredients in a food processor then process until well combined and become dough.
- Place the dough on a flat surface then roll until you have a rectangle with 1/4 –inch thick.
- Cut the dough into 1/2 –inch x 1/2 –inch squares then arranges them on the prepared baking pan.
- Bake for approximately 25 minutes until the squares are lightly brown.
- Transfer to a serving bowl and enjoy.

LUNCH: Simple Tomato Red Soup

Serving: 3

Nutrition Facts

Serving Size 14 g

Amount Per Serving

Calories 20

Calories from Fat 14

% Daily Value*

Total Fat 1.6g

2%

Cholesterol 0mg

0%

Sodium 3mg

0%

Potassium 38mg

1%

Total Carbohydrates 1.6g

1%

Sugars 0.6g

Protein 0.3g

Vitamin A 1%	•	Vitamin C 3%
Calcium 1%	•	Iron 1%

Nutrition Grade B

* Based on a 2000 calorie diet

Ingredients:
- 2 medium red tomatoes
- ¼ cup chopped onion
- 1 teaspoon minced garlic
- 1 teaspoon olive oil
- 1 teaspoon chopped parsley
- ¾ cup vegetable stock
- 1 teaspoon tomato paste
- ¼ teaspoon pepper powder

Instructions:
- Preheat an oven to 350 °F. Prepare a baking pan and line with parchment paper. Set aside.
- Cut the red tomatoes into wedges then arrange on the prepared baking pan.
- Place onion and minced garlic among the tomatoes then splash olive oil over the tomatoes and onion.
- Sprinkle pepper and chopped parsley on the top then bake for approximately 40 minutes. The tomatoes will reduce for approximately half their size.
- Remove the baked ingredients from the oven and set aside.
- Combine vegetable stock with tomato paste in a pan then bring to boil.
- Add the baked ingredients into the vegetable stock and bring to a simmer for approximately 10 minutes.
- Let it stand for a few minutes and when it is warm, transfer the mixture to a blender.
- Blend until smooth and incorporated and pour into a serving bowl.
- Garnish with fresh parsley on top then serve warm.

DINNER: Delicious Pork in Blanket

30 DAY PALEO CHALLENGE

Serving: 1

Nutrition Facts

Serving Size 0 g

Amount Per Serving

Calories 0

Calories from Fat 0

% Daily Value*

Total Fat 0.0g

0%

Cholesterol 0mg

0%

Sodium 0mg

0%

Potassium 0mg

0%

Total Carbohydrates 0.0g

0%

Protein 0.0g

Vitamin A 0%	•	Vitamin C 0%
Calcium 0%	•	Iron 0%

Nutrition Grade C+

* Based on a 2000 calorie diet

Ingredients:
- 1 lb. pork meat without fat
- 2 cups homemade barbecue sauce
- 12 slices bacon
- Fresh chopped lettuce, chopped cabbage, and lemon slices for garnish

Instructions:
- Cut the pork into 6 medium cubes then place in a bowl with a lid.
- Pour barbecue sauce over the cubed pork and marinate for at least 8 hours or overnight.
- Place two slices of bacon on a flat surface then put a cube of pork on the top of the bacon.
- Carefully wrap the pork with bacon then secure with a toothpicks.
- Repeat with the remaining ingredients.
- Preheat a grill over medium heat.
- Once it is hot, grill the wrapped pork then flips until the pork is no longer pink and completely cooked.
- Arrange the grilled pork on a serving dish and serve with fresh cabbage, lettuce, and lemon slice.
- Enjoy right away.

Day 24

BREAKFAST: Smooth Coconut Carrot Pudding

Serving: 3

Nutrition Facts
Serving Size 200 g

Amount Per Serving
Calories 49
Calories from Fat 27
% Daily Value*
Total Fat 3.0g
5%
Trans Fat 0.0g
Cholesterol 0mg
0%
Sodium 30mg
1%
Potassium 159mg
5%
Total Carbohydrates 4.5g
2%
Dietary Fiber 1.1g
4%
Sugars 1.8g
Protein 1.4g

Vitamin A 123%	•	Vitamin C 4%
Calcium 3%	•	Iron 2%

Nutrition Grade A
* Based on a 2000 calorie diet

Ingredients:
- 1 cup chopped carrots
- 2 cups water
- 3 teaspoons coconut butter
- 3 teaspoons almond butter
- ¼ teaspoon cinnamon powder
- ¼ teaspoon nutmeg powder

Instructions:
- Pour water in a pan and bring to boil.
- Once it is boiled, add in the chopped carrots then cook for approximately 15 minutes until tender.
- Drain the cooked carrots and place into a food processor.
- Add the remaining ingredients into the food processor then puree until smooth and creamy.
- Transfer the mixture to a serving bowl and enjoy right away.

LUNCH: Jalapeno Chicken in Lettuce Tacos

30 DAY PALEO CHALLENGE

Serving: 4

Nutrition Facts
Serving Size 104 g

Amount Per Serving
Calories 109
Calories from Fat 71
% Daily Value*
Total Fat 7.9g
12%
Saturated Fat 1.0g
5%
Trans Fat 0.0g
Cholesterol 16mg
5%
Sodium 143mg
6%
Potassium 227mg
6%
Total Carbohydrates 3.9g
1%
Dietary Fiber 1.0g
4%
Sugars 2.3g
Protein 6.8g

| Vitamin A 12% | • | Vitamin C 17% |
| Calcium 1% | • | Iron 4% |

Nutrition Grade B+
* Based on a 2000 calorie diet

Ingredients:
- ½ cup chicken strips
- 2 tablespoons olive oil
- ¼ cup chopped onion
- 1 ½ cup chopped tomatoes
- 1 tablespoon jalapeno chili
- ½ teaspoon cumin
- ¼ teaspoon brown sugar
- ¼ teaspoon sea salt
- ¼ teaspoon pepper powder
- Fresh lettuce leaves, for the tacos
- 1 tablespoon chopped leek
- 1 tablespoon sliced jalapeno chilies

Instructions:
- Preheat a skillet then pour olive oil into the skillet.
- Once it is hot, stir in chicken strips and fry until golden brown. Set aside.
- In the same skillet, sauté the chopped onion until wilted and aromatic then add chopped tomatoes, jalapeno chilies, cumin, brown sugar, sea salt, and pepper powder. Bring to a simmer for approximately 15 minutes until the mixture is thicken.
- Return the chicken into the sauce and cook for another 5 minutes.
- Prepare a fresh lettuce on a flat surface then put a scoop of cooked chicken and sauce on the lettuce.
- Sprinkle chopped leek and sliced jalapeno chili then carefully wrap with the lettuce.
- Repeat to the remaining lettuce and chicken and arrange on a serving dish.
- Serve and enjoy.

DINNER: Scrumptious Spicy Paleo Pork Ribs

30 DAY PALEO CHALLENGE

Serving: 1

Nutrition Facts

Serving Size 148 g

Amount Per Serving

Calories 901

Calories from Fat 901

% Daily Value*

Total Fat 101.7g

156%

Saturated Fat 14.6g

73%

Cholesterol 0mg

0%

Sodium 29mg

1%

Potassium 185mg

5%

Total Carbohydrates 7.7g

3%

Dietary Fiber 3.1g

12%

Sugars 1.7g

Protein 1.4g

Vitamin A 40%	•	Vitamin C 13%
Calcium 5%	•	Iron 9%

Nutrition Grade D+

Ingredients:
- 2 lb. pork rib without fat
- ½ tablespoon minced garlic
- ¼ cup chopped onion
- 1 teaspoon paprika
- 1 teaspoon coriander
- 1 teaspoon oregano
- 1 teaspoon red chili powder
- ½ cup olive oil
- ½ teaspoon cinnamon powder
- Lemon slices, for garnish

Instructions:
- Combine minced garlic, chopped onion, paprika, coriander, oregano, and red chili powder in a bowl. Stir until incorporated.
- Rub the pork rib with the mixture and marinate for approximately 30 minutes.
- Preheat an oven to 300 °F and prepare a baking pan.
- Wrap the marinated pork rib with aluminum foil then place on the baking pan and bake for 60 minutes.
- Meanwhile, combine the olive oil with cinnamon powder, set aside.
- Remove the cooked pork rib from the oven and discard the aluminum foil.
- Grease the cooked pork with applesauce mixture then return into the oven and bake for another 30 minutes.
- Once it is done, remove from the oven then transfer to a serving dish.
- Garnish with lemon slices then serve hot.

Day 25

BREAKFAST: The Nutritious Spinach Omelet

30 DAY PALEO CHALLENGE

Serving: 4

Nutrition Facts
Serving Size 43 g

Amount Per Serving
Calories 47
Calories from Fat 32
% Daily Value*
Total Fat 3.6g
5%
Saturated Fat 0.5g
3%
Trans Fat 0.0g
Cholesterol 0mg
0%
Sodium 23mg
1%
Potassium 93mg
3%
Total Carbohydrates 2.0g
1%
Sugars 0.8g
Protein 2.2g

Vitamin A 14%	•	Vitamin C 6%
Calcium 1%	•	Iron 1%

Nutrition Grade B
* Based on a 2000 calorie diet

Ingredients:
- 1 tablespoon olive oil
- ½ cup chopped onion
- 1 teaspoon minced garlic
- 1 cup chopped spinach
- 2 organic egg whites
- ¼ teaspoon black pepper powder

Instructions:
- Preheat a skillet over medium heat then pour olive oil into the skillet.
- Once it is hot, stir in chopped onion and dice garlic into the skillet then sauté until wilted and lightly golden brown. Set aside.
- Place the egg whites and beat them in a medium bowl. After that, put the sautéed onion and garlic then add the remaining ingredients into the beaten eggs.
- Preheat an oven to 350 °°F and line a baking pan with parchment paper.
- Pour the egg mixture into the prepared baking pan and bake for approximately 15 minutes until lightly brown.
- Transfer the baked omelet to a serving dish then serve immediately.
- Best to be enjoyed with tomato sauce.

LUNCH: Red and Green Paleo Salads

30 DAY PALEO CHALLENGE

Serving: 3

Nutrition Facts
Serving Size 124 g

Amount Per Serving
Calories 103
Calories from Fat 86
% Daily Value*
Total Fat 9.6g
15%
Saturated Fat 1.4g
7%
Trans Fat 0.0g
Cholesterol 0mg
0%
Sodium 3mg
0%
Potassium 186mg
5%
Total Carbohydrates 5.0g
2%
Dietary Fiber 1.2g
5%
Sugars 1.8g
Protein 0.9g

| Vitamin A 5% | • | Vitamin C 7% |
| Calcium 4% | • | Iron 6% |

Nutrition Grade C+

Ingredients:

- 1 teaspoon minced garlic
- 3 teaspoons sliced basil
- 3 teaspoons chopped oregano
- 1 medium cucumber
- 2 tablespoons chopped red tomato
- 2 tablespoons balsamic vinegar
- 2 tablespoons olive oil
- 1 teaspoon black pepper powder

Instructions:

- Cut the cucumber into cubes and discard the seeds. Set aside.
- Toss the cubed cucumber, tomato, minced garlic, sliced basil, and chopped oregano in a salad bowl.
- Drizzle balsamic vinegar and olive oil over the vegetable mixture then sprinkle black pepper powder on top.
- Serve and enjoy.

DINNER: Original Beef Patties with Scrumptious Sauce

30 DAY PALEO CHALLENGE

Serving: 1

Nutrition Facts
Serving Size 552 g

Amount Per Serving

Calories 1,905
Calories from Fat 1905

% Daily Value*

Total Fat 211.7g

326%

Saturated Fat 30.4g

152%

Trans Fat 0.0g

Cholesterol 0mg

0%

Sodium 71mg

3%

Potassium 594mg

17%

Total Carbohydrates 20.4g

7%

Dietary Fiber 5.2g

21%

Sugars 8.4g

Protein 4.5g

Vitamin A 7%	•	Vitamin C 24%
Calcium 19%	•	Iron 19%

Nutrition Grade D

Ingredients:
PATTIES
- ¼ cup chopped onion
- 1 teaspoon olive oil
- 1 cup minced beef
- ¼ cup grated beetroot
- 1 teaspoon diced garlic
- 1 tablespoon chopped rosemary
- 1 teaspoon black pepper powder
- 1 cup olive oil, for frying
- 1 cup sliced cucumber

CUCUMBER SALADS
- 1 cup sliced cucumber
- 1 teaspoon lemon zest
- 3 teaspoons sesame seeds
- 2 tablespoons apple cider vinegar
- ½ teaspoon Dijon mustard
- ¼ teaspoon black pepper powder

GARNISH
- Fresh lettuce
- Fresh parsley

Instructions:
- Preheat a skillet then pour olive oil into the skillet.
- Once it is hot, stir in onion and sauté until wilted and aromatic.
- Place the sautéed onion together with the patties ingredients in a bowl and mix well.
- Using your hands, mold the mixture into small patties.
- Preheat a frying pan then pour a cup of olive oil into the pan.

- Once it is hot, arrange the patties on the pan and cook for approximately 6 minutes.
- Carefully flip the patties and cook another side for 6 minutes as well—the beetroot can easily burn so avoid high heat in frying the patties.
- Once the patties are cooked, remove from the pan and let them cool for a few minutes.
- Meanwhile, combine the salad ingredients in a bowl and mix until incorporated.
- Arrange fresh lettuce on a serving dish then put the patties on the lettuce.
- Drizzle sauce over the patties and garnish with fresh parsley.
- Serve and enjoy at dinner.

Day 26

BREAKFAST: Delicious Coconut Pancake with Strawberry Sauce

30 DAY PALEO CHALLENGE

Serving: 6

Nutrition Facts
Serving Size 21 g

Amount Per Serving
Calories 24
Calories from Fat 21
% Daily Value*
Total Fat 2.4g
4%
Trans Fat 0.0g
Cholesterol 0mg
0%
Sodium 1mg
0%
Potassium 61mg
2%
Total Carbohydrates 1.1g
0%
Sugars 0.6g
Protein 0.1g

Vitamin A 0% •	Vitamin C 12%
Calcium 2% •	Iron 0%

Nutrition Grade C+
* Based on a 2000 calorie diet

Ingredients:
- ¼ cup coconut flour
- 4 fresh organic eggs white
- 2 ½ tablespoons water
- 3 teaspoons olive oil
- ½ teaspoon baking powder
- ¼ teaspoon apple cider vinegar
- ½ cup fresh strawberries
- Fresh strawberries, for garnish

Instructions:
- Combine coconut flour and eggs whites in a bowl.
- Using a hand mixer beat them until smooth and creamy then adds water and olive oil into the mixture.
- Meanwhile, preheat a saucepan over low heat.
- Stir in baking powder and apple cider vinegar a few seconds before pouring the mixture into the hot saucepan.
- Take about ¼ cup of the mixture and pour into the hot saucepan. Cook for approximately 30 seconds then flip the pancake.
- Make sure that both sides of the pancake are lightly golden brown.
- Repeat to the remaining mixture and set aside.
- After that, place fresh strawberries in a blender then blend on high speed until creamy and incorporated.
- Put a pancake on a serving dish and coat with strawberry sauce.
- Cover with another pancake and repeat with the remaining pancakes and strawberry sauce.
- Garnish with fresh strawberries and serve immediately.

LUNCH: Energetic Veggie Tuna Salads

Servings: 4

Nutrition Facts

Serving Size 11 g

Amount Per Serving

Calories 3

Calories from Fat 0

% Daily Value*

Total Fat 0.0g

0%

Trans Fat 0.0g

Cholesterol 0mg

0%

Sodium 7mg

0%

Potassium 40mg

1%

Total Carbohydrates 0.7g

0%

Protein 0.2g

Vitamin A 7%	•	Vitamin C 9%
Calcium 1%	•	Iron 1%

Nutrition Grade A

* Based on a 2000 calorie diet

Ingredients:
- ¼ cup cooked tuna chunks
- ¼ cup chopped celery
- ¼ cup chopped parsley
- 1 teaspoon minced garlic
- ½ teaspoon black pepper powder

Instructions:
- Place all ingredients in a salad bowl.
- Using a fork mix all ingredients until combined.
- Cover the salad bowl with a lid then chill in the refrigerator for at least an hour or more.
- Enjoy cold.

DINNER: Traditional Indian Curry

Serving: 3

Nutrition Facts
Serving Size 154 g

Amount Per Serving

Calories 159

Calories from Fat 70

% Daily Value*

Total Fat 7.8g

12%

Saturated Fat 2.6g

13%

Trans Fat 0.0g

Cholesterol 43mg

14%

Sodium 317mg

13%

Potassium 303mg

9%

Total Carbohydrates 3.7g

1%

Dietary Fiber 0.9g

4%

Sugars 1.4g

Protein 19.0g

Vitamin A 2%	•	Vitamin C 3%
Calcium 3%	•	Iron 8%

Nutrition Grade B

* Based on a 2000 calorie diet

Ingredients:

- 1 teaspoon olive oil
- 1 tablespoon chopped onion
- ¼ teaspoon pepper powder
- ½ cup cubed sweet potatoes
- 1 teaspoon curry powder
- 1 teaspoon tomato paste
- ½ teaspoon ginger powder
- 1 ½ teaspoons garlic powder
- 1 cup chicken broth
- ½ tablespoon tomato
- 2 tablespoons coconut milk
- 1 cup chopped chicken breast
- 1 ½ teaspoons almond butter
- 2 tablespoons cilantro

Instructions:

- Preheat olive oil in a skillet then stir in chopped onion. Sauté until wilted and aromatic then add the cubed sweet potatoes into the skillet.
- Stir until the sweet potatoes soften and season with pepper powder.
- Add curry powder, tomato paste, ginger powder, and garlic powder into the skillet then pour chicken broth over the seasoned sweet potatoes.
- Put chopped chicken breast into the skillet together with the almond butter and cilantro.
- Bring to boil and stir until the chicken is completely cooked.
- Transfer the curry to a serving bowl and serve warm.

Day 27

BREAKFAST: Scrumptious Macadamia Paleo Waffles

Serving: 5

Nutrition Facts
Serving Size 23 g

Amount Per Serving

Calories 56
Calories from Fat 52
% Daily Value*
Total Fat 5.8g
9%
Saturated Fat 0.9g
4%
Cholesterol 0mg
0%
Sodium 58mg
2%
Potassium 30mg
1%
Total Carbohydrates 0.8g
0%
Protein 1.0g

Vitamin A 0%   •   Vitamin C 0%
Calcium 1%   •   Iron 1%
Nutrition Grade C+

* Based on a 2000 calorie diet

Nutrition Facts

Serving Size 23 g

Ingredients:

- 1 organic egg white
- 4 tablespoons chopped macadamia nuts
- 2 teaspoons olive oil
- 3 teaspoons coconut flour
- ¼ teaspoon baking soda
- ¼ cup water

Instructions:

- Place all of the ingredients in a bowl. Using a hand mixer beat until smooth and incorporated.
- Preheat a waffle iron over low heat then pour the mixture into the hot waffle iron.
- Cook for approximately 45 minutes then transfer the waffles to a serving dish..
- Best to be served with unsweetened fruit juice as healthy breakfast.

LUNCH: Delicious Paleo Chicken With Sweet Potato Chips

30 DAY PALEO CHALLENGE

Serving: 2

Nutrition Facts
Serving Size 210 g

Amount Per Serving
Calories 720
Calories from Fat 536
% Daily Value*
Total Fat 59.5g
92%
Saturated Fat 13.7g
69%
Cholesterol 54mg
18%
Sodium 1001mg
42%
Potassium 419mg
12%
Total Carbohydrates 29.4g
10%
Dietary Fiber 2.5g
10%
Sugars 4.5g
Protein 21.6g

Vitamin A 8%	•	Vitamin C 32%
Calcium 2%	•	Iron 18%

Nutrition Grade C
* Based on a 2000 calorie diet

Ingredients:
POTATO CHIPS
- 1 medium sweet potato
- 3 teaspoons olive oil
- 1 teaspoon chopped rosemary
- ½ teaspoon sea salt

CRISPY CHICKEN
- 1 cup chopped chicken
- 4 tablespoons tapioca starch
- ½ teaspoon sea salt
- ¼ teaspoon black pepper powder
- ¼ teaspoon paprika
- ¼ teaspoon garlic powder
- ½ cup olive oil

Instructions:
- Preheat an oven to 375 °F. Prepare a baking pan then line with parchment paper. Set aside.
- Peel the sweet potato and slice thinly using a very sharp knife.
- Season the sliced sweet potato with olive oil, chopped rosemary, and sea salt.
- Arrange the sweet potato on the prepared baking pan then bake for about 10 minutes.
- Flip each sliced potato and return to the oven for another 10 minutes. The sweet potato chips will look golden brown.
- Transfer the sweet potato chips to a bowl then set aside.
- Reduce the oven to 350 °F. Prepare another baking pan and line with parchment paper. Set aside.
- Combine tapioca starch, sea salt, black pepper powder,

paprika, and garlic powder in bowl. Stir well.
- Coat the chicken with the mixture then refrigerate for approximately 15 minutes.
- Preheat a skillet then pour olive oil into the skillet.
- Once it is hot, fry the coated chicken for about 3 minutes.
- Flip the chicken and fry for another 3 minutes until both sides of the chicken are golden brown.
- Transfer the fried chicken on the prepared baking pan and bake for about 20 minutes.
- Arrange the baked chicken and potato chips in a lunch box and enjoy at lunch.

DINNER: Spiced Beef Stew with Carrots and Blueberries

30 DAY PALEO CHALLENGE

Serving: 3

Nutrition Facts

Serving Size 96 g

Amount Per Serving

Calories 152

Calories from Fat 112

% Daily Value*

Total Fat 12.4g

19%

Saturated Fat 1.6g

8%

Trans Fat 0.0g

Cholesterol 0mg

0%

Sodium 182mg

8%

Potassium 209mg

6%

Total Carbohydrates 10.1g

3%

Dietary Fiber 2.2g

9%

Sugars 5.1g

Protein 1.9g

Vitamin A 123%	•	Vitamin C 12%
Calcium 3%	•	Iron 4%

Nutrition Grade B+

* Based on a 2000 calorie diet

Ingredients:
- 2 cups chopped beef
- ½ cup fresh blueberries
- 1 cup chopped carrots
- 1 tablespoon almond butter
- 2 tablespoons olive oil
- ¼ teaspoon sea salt
- ¼ teaspoon black pepper
- ¼ teaspoon garlic powder
- ½ cup sliced onion

Instructions:
- Preheat a skillet then pour olive oil into the skillet.
- Once it is hot, stir in chopped beef and onion then sauté until the onion is aromatic and the beef is wilted.
- Season the beef with sea salt, black pepper powder, and garlic powder.
- Add the chopped carrots and cook stir until cooked.
- Last, add in the blueberries and butter then stir until the butter melts.
- Transfer the cooked beef to a serving dish and serve warm.

Day 28

BREAKFAST: Delectable Ginger Banana Paleo Bars

30 DAY PALEO CHALLENGE

Serving: 8

Nutrition Facts
Serving Size 20 g

Amount Per Serving
Calories 52
Calories from Fat 39
% Daily Value*
Total Fat 4.3g
7%
Cholesterol 0mg
0%
Sodium 80mg
3%
Potassium 57mg
2%
Total Carbohydrates 3.6g
1%
Sugars 1.8g
Protein 0.2g

| Vitamin A 0% | • | Vitamin C 2% |
| Calcium 0% | • | Iron 0% |

Nutrition Grade C+

Based on a 2000 calorie diet

Nutrition Facts
Serving Size 20 g

Ingredients:
- 1 medium ripe banana
- ½ cup almond flour
- 2 ½ tablespoons almond oil
- 3 organic eggs whites
- ¾ teaspoon ginger powder
- 1 teaspoon cinnamon powder
- ½ teaspoon cardamom
- ½ teaspoon baking soda

Instructions:
- Preheat an oven to 350 °F and line a small baking pan with parchment paper.
- Peel the banana and cut into slices.
- Place the sliced banana in a food processor together with almond oil, eggs whites, ginger powder, cinnamon powder, and cardamom. Process until smooth and incorporated.
- Add in the baking soda then quickly stir until well combined.
- Pour the mixture into the prepared baking pan and bake for approximately 30 minutes.
- Once it is done, remove from the oven and let it cool for about 30 minutes.
- Cut into bars and arrange on a serving dish.
- Serve and enjoy.

LUNCH: Paleo Salads in Jar

Serving: 2

Nutrition Facts

Serving Size 144 g

Amount Per Serving

Calories 100

Calories from Fat 45

% Daily Value*

Total Fat 5.0g

8%

Saturated Fat 0.9g

4%

Trans Fat 0.0g

Cholesterol 16mg

5%

Sodium 135mg

6%

Potassium 329mg

9%

Total Carbohydrates 8.2g

3%

Dietary Fiber 2.1g

9%

Sugars 4.0g

Protein 6.3g

Vitamin A 112%	•	Vitamin C 60%
Calcium 3%	•	Iron 7%

Nutrition Grade A

* Based on a 2000 calorie diet

Ingredients:
- 1 ½ teaspoons olive oil
- ¼ cup chopped chicken fillet
- ½ cup sliced carrots
- ½ cup sliced bell pepper
- ¼ cup chopped onion
- 1 teaspoon minced garlic
- ¼ cup mashed avocado
- 1 tablespoon lime juice
- 2 tablespoons salsa
- 2 tablespoons chopped tomato
- ½ cup cubed cucumber
- ¼ cup chopped cilantro
- 1 cup chopped fresh lettuce

Instructions
- Preheat a skillet then pour half of the olive oil into the skillet.
- Once it is hot, stir in chopped chicken fillet and cook until golden brown.
- Set aside.
- In the same skillet, pour the remaining olive oil then cooks the sliced carrot until tender.
- Add the sliced bell pepper, onion, and garlic then sauté for a few minutes. Turn the stove off.
- Combine mashed avocado and lime juice until incorporated then set aside.
- Place salsa in the bottom of the jar and spread evenly.
- Layer with avocado mixture, continued with cooked vegetables, then put chicken over the vegetables.
- Add chopped tomato and cucumber then place cilantro

and fresh lettuce on top.
- Cover the jar with the lid then refrigerate until you want to consume it.
- Enjoy!

DINNER: Grilled Chicken Spicy

30 DAY PALEO CHALLENGE

Servings: 2

Nutrition Facts

Serving Size 350 g

Amount Per Serving

Calories 1,286

Calories from Fat 1018

% Daily Value*

Total Fat 113.1g

174%

Saturated Fat 15.0g

75%

Trans Fat 0.0g

Cholesterol 194mg

65%

Sodium 981mg

41%

Potassium 719mg

21%

Total Carbohydrates 4.0g

1%

Dietary Fiber 2.0g

8%

Sugars 0.8g

Protein 73.8g

Vitamin A 45%	•	Vitamin C 8%
Calcium 5%	•	Iron 23%

Nutrition Grade C+

* Based on a 2000 calorie diet

Ingredients:
- 1 lb. chicken breast
- 1 cup olive oil, to fry
- 1 tablespoon sweet paprika
- 1 teaspoon chili powder
- ¾ teaspoon sea salt
- ½ teaspoon allspice
- 1 teaspoon black pepper powder
- 1 ½ teaspoon olive oil
- 1 teaspoon minced garlic
- 1 teaspoon tomato paste
- 1 tablespoon lime juice
- Lemon slices, for garnish

Instructions:
- Cut the chicken breast into slices. Set aside.
- Place sweet paprika, chili powder, sea salt, allspice, black pepper powder, olive oil, minced garlic, tomato paste, and lime juice in a bowl. Stir well.
- Add the chicken into the mixture and marinate for at least 30 minutes.
- Preheat a grill over medium heat. Once it is hot, cook the chicken for approximately 4 minutes then flips it. Make sure that both sides of the chicken are golden brown.
- Remove the chicken from the grill and transfer to a serving dish.
- Garnish with lemon slices and enjoy.

Day 29

BREAKFAST: Spicy Vegetable Casserole

Serving: 6

Nutrition Facts
Serving Size 27 g

Amount Per Serving
Calories 16
Calories from Fat 7
% Daily Value*
Total Fat 0.8g
1%
Trans Fat 0.0g
Cholesterol 0mg
0%
Sodium 17mg
1%
Potassium 71mg
2%
Total Carbohydrates 1.9g
1%
Dietary Fiber 0.6g
2%
Sugars 0.6g
Protein 0.5g

Vitamin A 12%   Vitamin C 18%
Calcium 1%   Iron 2%
Nutrition Grade A

* Based on a 2000 calorie diet
Nutrition Facts

Ingredients:
- 1 cup chopped spinach
- ½ cup broccoli florets
- 1 teaspoon olive oil
- ½ cup chopped onion
- 1 tablespoon chopped green chili
- 1 teaspoon minced garlic
- 2 organic eggs whites, lightly beaten
- ¼ teaspoon black pepper powder
- 1 tablespoon chopped parsley, for garnish

Instructions:
- Preheat an oven to 375 °F and grease a small casserole dish with cooking spray.
- Preheat a skillet then pour olive oil into the skillet.
- Once it is hot, stir in chopped onion, minced garlic and green chilies into the skillet and sauté until wilted and aromatic.
- Transfer the sautéed onion mixture to the beaten eggs then season with black pepper powder.
- Add the chopped spinach and broccoli florets into the egg mixture and stir well.
- Pour the mixture into the prepared casserole dish then bake for approximately 45 minutes.
- Once it is cooked, remove the casserole from the oven and let it cool for about five minutes.
- Sprinkle chopped parsley on the top for garnish.
- Serve and enjoy warm.

LUNCH: Original Steamed Broccoli

30 DAY PALEO CHALLENGE

Serving: 1

Nutrition Facts
Serving Size 142 g

Amount Per Serving
Calories 325
Calories from Fat 232
% Daily Value*
Total Fat 25.7g
40%
Saturated Fat 2.2g
11%
Trans Fat 0.0g
Cholesterol 0mg
0%
Sodium 31mg
1%
Potassium 655mg
19%
Total Carbohydrates 16.3g
5%
Dietary Fiber 6.3g
25%
Sugars 2.6g
Protein 12.8g

| Vitamin A 11% | • | Vitamin C 137% |
| Calcium 18% | • | Iron 14% |

Nutrition Grade A-
* Based on a 2000 calorie diet

278

Ingredients:
- 1 cup broccoli florets
- 1 teaspoon minced garlic
- 4 tablespoons chopped almonds
- 1 ½ tablespoons almond butter

Instructions:
- Pour water in a small saucepan and bring to boil.
- Once it is boiled, toss in the broccoli and cook for a few seconds. Drain and place in a bowl.
- Preheat the saucepan over medium heat then stir in almond butter, minced garlic, and chopped almonds.
- Sauté them well until the almond butter melts and the garlic is lightly golden brown.
- Drizzle almond butter on the top of the broccoli and serve right away.

DINNER: Delicious Simple Baked Salmon

Serving: 2

Nutrition Facts
Serving Size 244 g

Amount Per Serving
Calories 365
Calories from Fat 190
% Daily Value*
Total Fat 21.1g
33%
Saturated Fat 3.1g
15%
Trans Fat 0.0g
Cholesterol 100mg
33%
Sodium 336mg
14%
Potassium 889mg
25%
Total Carbohydrates 0.8g
0%
Protein 44.2g

Vitamin A 5%   •   Vitamin C 7%
Calcium 10%   •   Iron 15%
Nutrition Grade C+
* Based on a 2000 calorie diet

Ingredients:
- 1 lb. salmon fillet
- 1 tablespoon lemon juice
- ¼ teaspoon sea salt
- ¼ teaspoon black pepper powder
- 2 teaspoons chopped thyme
- 1 tablespoon olive oil

Instructions:
- Preheat an oven to 400 °F then lines a baking pan with parchment paper.
- Place salmon on the prepared baking pan then season with salt and black pepper.
- Next, splash lemon juice over the salmon and sprinkle thyme on top.
- After that, drizzle with olive oil and bake for approximately 25 minutes.
- Once it is done, remove the cooked salmon from the oven then transfer to a serving dish.
- Serve immediately.

Day 30

BREAKFAST: Paleo Simple Almond Muffin

Serving: 4

Nutrition Facts
Serving Size 18 g

Amount Per Serving
Calories 65
Calories from Fat 61
% Daily Value*
Total Fat 6.8g
10%
Saturated Fat 0.6g
3%
Trans Fat 0.0g
Cholesterol 0mg
0%
Sodium 88mg
4%
Potassium 16mg
0%
Total Carbohydrates 0.3g
0%
Protein 0.9g

Vitamin A 0%   Vitamin C 0%
Calcium 0%   Iron 0%
Nutrition Grade D+
* Based on a 2000 calorie diet
Nutrition Facts

Ingredients:

- 2 tablespoons almond flour
- 2 tablespoons almond oil
- 1 organic egg white
- 1 ½ teaspoons unsweetened apple juice
- ¼ teaspoon baking soda
- ½ teaspoon apple cider vinegar
- Roasted sliced almonds, for garnish

Instructions:

- Preheat an oven to 350 °F and prepare 3 muffin paper cups.
- Place almond flour, almond oil, and egg whites in a bowl. Stir until smooth and incorporated.
- Pour unsweetened apple juice into the mixture then baking soda, and apple cider vinegar into the mixture.
- Stir until well combined then divide the mixture into 3 muffin paper cups.
- Sprinkle sliced almond on the top then bake for approximately 20 minutes or until a toothpick comes out clean.
- Remove the muffins from the oven and let them cool for about 30 minutes.
- Serve and enjoy.

LUNCH: Nutritious Mixed Salads

30 DAY PALEO CHALLENGE

Serving: 3

Nutrition Facts
Serving Size 66 g

Amount Per Serving
Calories 31
Calories from Fat 2
% Daily Value*
Total Fat 0.2g
0%
Trans Fat 0.0g
Cholesterol 0mg
0%
Sodium 165mg
7%
Potassium 122mg
3%
Total Carbohydrates 7.7g
3%
Dietary Fiber 1.0g
4%
Sugars 5.5g
Protein 0.6g

Vitamin A 19%   •   Vitamin C 49%
Calcium 2%   •   Iron 4%
Nutrition Grade A
* Based on a 2000 calorie diet

Ingredients:
- 1 cup chopped spinach
- 1 cup shredded sea bass
- 1 cup chopped pineapple
- ½ cup chopped half ripe papaya
- ½ teaspoon cumin
- ¼ teaspoon black pepper powder

Instructions:
- Steam the bass until cooked then set aside.
- Layer spinach, pineapple, papaya, and steamed sea bass in a salad bowl.
- Season with cumin and pepper then serve right away.

DINNER: Spicy Chicken Kebab

30 DAY PALEO CHALLENGE

Serving: 2

Nutrition Facts
Serving Size 40 g

Amount Per Serving
Calories 237
Calories from Fat 230
% Daily Value*
Total Fat 25.5g
39%
Saturated Fat 3.6g
18%
Trans Fat 0.0g
Cholesterol 0mg
0%
Sodium 85mg
4%
Potassium 14mg
0%
Total Carbohydrates 4.8g
2%
Sugars 4.4g
Protein 0.4g

Vitamin A 0%	•	Vitamin C 0%
Calcium 0%	•	Iron 1%

Nutrition Grade D
* Based on a 2000 calorie diet

Ingredients:
- 1 lb. boneless chicken breast without fat
- ¼ cup olive oil
- 3 teaspoons yellow mustard
- ½ tablespoon raw honey
- Lemon slices, for garnish
- Lettuce, for garnish

Instructions:
- Combine olive oil, yellow mustard, and raw honey in a bowl.
- Cut the boneless chicken into cubes.
- Skewer the cubed chicken with wooden skewers then grease with the sauce.
- Preheat a grill pan and once it is hot, grill the chicken over medium heat until completely cooked.
- Repeat to grease the chicken with sauce during the grilling process.
- Arrange the grilled chicken on a serving dish and garnish with fresh lettuce and sliced lemon.
- Serve and enjoy warm.